MW01608915

FearLESS Retirement

A Simple, Effective & Powerful Approach
to Your Best Retirement

Matthew J. Curfman, CFP®
Richmond Brothers, Inc.

Matthew J. Curfman/Richmond Brothers, Inc.
3568 Wildwood Ave.
Jackson, Michigan 49202
www.richmondbrothers.com/FearLESS

Book layout ©2023 Advisors Excel, LLC

FearLESS Retirement: A Simple, Effective, & Powerful Approach to Your Best Retirement/Matthew J. Curfman.

ISBN 9798860696747

"Don't look for the needle in the haystack. Just buy the haystack."

~ JACK BOGLE, Founder/CEO of The Vanguard Group

"The stock market is designed to transfer money from the active to the patient."

~ WARREN BUFFET, American Business Magnate

"Tell me and I forget. Teach me and I may remember. Involve me and I learn."

~ BENJAMIN FRANKLIN, Founding Father

"A genius is the man who can do the average thing when everyone else around him is losing his mind."

~ NAPOLEAN, Military Commander and Political Leader

For Greg & Shirlee Curfman, who taught me the value of education and hard work.

For David Richmond, who led my financial education beyond school and university and helped me to dream.

Finally, for my teachers and mentors, especially Mrs. Shafer.

Table of Contents

The Importance of Planning

Have you ever looked at your friend, neighbor, or work colleague and admired how they seem to have all their ducks in a row regarding their financial plans and investments? You wish you could be more like them.

I've had the opportunity to sit down with many individuals and families over the last two decades and "look under the hood," so to speak. Trust me when I say true wealth is what you *don't* see. It's the money not spent on expensive things like big houses, flashy cars, timeshares, and vacation homes. So please, don't fall victim to the idea that you should have started earlier or know more than you think you do.

In 2007, I worked with eight couples living in the same neighborhood. As I sat down with them throughout the year, I was fascinated to learn their thoughts about their friends' and neighbors' wealth compared to their own. It was the perfect example of how appearances can be deceiving. The couple—we'll call them Bob and Sue—with the most assets did not own the biggest house, drive luxury cars, or take fancy European vacations. They were not CEOs, COOs, or CFOs with huge compensation packages and stock options. They were everyday people like you and me.

To be fair, they drove nice cars and had a nice, well-maintained home. They took vacations and helped their two older children through college and their youngest through trade school. Interestingly, the youngest became an electrician and earned more than his college-educated siblings.

What did Bob and Sue do that allowed them to amass more than $2.5 million in retirement funds? Throughout their thirty-year careers, they paid themselves first and lived on whatever was left. It sounds simple, but they made tough decisions that not everyone is willing to make. No matter what was happening in the economy or the markets, they consistently saved into their 401(k)s with every paycheck for over thirty years.

You might be wondering, if Bob and Sue were so successful in building their wealth, why did they want to sit down with me? Simple. They were excellent at saving but didn't know what their next step should be. After thirty-plus years of dreaming about retirement, they weren't confident they had the knowledge and resources to pull everything together. It's funny how realizing your dream can be scary and maybe even overwhelm you with fear about what comes next.

Bob and Sue's biggest fear was outliving their money: a very common fear. How does it work when we're no longer adding to our investments and taking withdrawals instead? What if the economy goes into recession? When working, we still have a paycheck and don't have to depend on our portfolio for income. When that paycheck goes away, it can be scary.

Bob, Sue, and I had open and honest conversations about their goals, retirement dreams, and the fears that came with them. These conversations were critical in helping me understand what was keeping them up at night and why retirement had become so scary for them. They realized they needed help and guidance to feel comfortable taking the final step to realizing their retirement dream. I had the privilege of sharing the knowledge, wisdom, and guidance they needed based on my years helping others cross that same bridge and confront those fears and concerns standing in the way of their dreams.

At Richmond Brothers, Inc., we believe in being trusted partners with our clients. Together, Bob, Sue, and I created a solid retirement income plan, allowing them to confidently move forward into that future they'd been waiting for.

Consider the Source

There is much more to retirement planning than having a diversified portfolio or amassing a huge nest egg. Sure, the nest egg is significant, but many other factors are at play—some you may be aware of, and some you may not be. My mentor, Ed Slott, often says, "You don't know what you don't know"—an extremely simple yet powerful idea.

Choose carefully where you get your financial advice from. There are numerous resources and many great financial planners and advisors you could work with. I advocate for working with professionals when you have identified an important area in which you are not an expert. For example, I know a lot about taxes, especially for investments and retirement accounts. Yet, I choose to use a CPA or an accounting firm to help guide me with my personal and business taxes because I'm not an expert in those areas.

While there are many great resources, there are just as many questionable ones. I can't tell you how often I've heard someone mention a friend, relative, or neighbor who recommended they buy a certain stock, or how they watched a financial show on television and heard from the host how a certain stock would be worthwhile to own.

The bottom line is, do you know your risk tolerance? Does the person who recommended the stock know your financial circumstances and plan? Do they know your risk tolerance? Does every single one of the millions of viewers of some TV show fall in the exact same category? I think you can see where I'm going with this.

You don't know what you don't know, so it's important to seek guidance from a trusted source who is also familiar with your specific situation and needs.

My clients often remark that my team and I have a way of explaining and simplifying incredibly complex financial topics in a way that makes sense for them. That's why I wrote this book. Whether you are planning for your upcoming retirement or you've been retired for several years and simply want a reassessment, this book is for you. My goal is to help educate and guide you along your financial journey so you can move closer to your goals without fear. That's also why we created the FearLess Financial Approach™, an outline of the guidance we provide at Richmond Brothers, Inc. You can learn more by visiting our website:

www.richmondbrothers.com/FearLESS

Financial GPS

There will be unknowns in retirement. Many people will be in retirement between fifteen and forty years. Think back on your last thirty years; did anything unexpected happen with your life, finances, or family? Of course it did. Dealing with the unexpected is part of the human experience. Working with a professional financial planner can help alleviate some of the worries that come with the unexpected.

Let's imagine you've lived in Michigan your whole life but have a dream of traveling to San Diego. Before retirement, you never had enough vacation time to fulfill that dream. Now is the time, but there's just one problem: You're deathly afraid of flying. Now that you're retired, you could drive there. It may take longer, but that's okay. Would you get in your car and just drive west, blindly hoping you end up in San Diego? Probably not. You would likely use Google Maps or another app to set a specific location (such as a hotel) to plot your course.

This might be an oversimplified analogy, but I think you get my point. Think of me as your financial GPS helping you get from where you are now to where you want to be. Use the people and resources available to create a plan, alleviate your fears, and fulfill your dream. It can be done!

In the following pages, we'll discuss some of the resources for creating a FearLess retirement and some of the challenges you may face along the way. Some of what we cover might sound scary at first, but with the right guidance and information, you'll have the power to turn your retirement dreams into reality.

Let's get started!

Potential Risks to Your Ideal Retirement

Ever feel like life gets in the way and prevents you from doing things you should not ignore? I think if we're honest with ourselves, we've all put off obligations we know are important.

In your case, you may be reading this book because it's time to get serious about financial planning and, specifically, devising a way to best prepare for retirement. A retirement plan should be based on more components than just your investments or your finances. The preparation of that strategy begins with your desires, ambitions, and goals for this fulfilling season of life.

There's no such thing as a silly question. Not when one of the most common questions we hear from folks regarding retirement is, "Am I going to be okay?" Often, it seems, people are reluctant to meet with financial professionals because they worry they might sound uneducated. Yet, it's understandable for you to be a novice when it comes to financial issues and retirement concerns. You've been busy with your lives and your careers. Time spent away from work has meant time spent being around those you love and engaging in the activities you enjoy. Retirement provides the opportunity to do even more of that, while not fretting over work obligations.

Concerns people have about what they may encounter during retirement can be far-reaching and still perfectly legitimate. For a quick snapshot, I want to provide a brief sampling of wide-ranging issues that can come up during discussions about what to potentially brace for in retirement. This book will touch on many of these issues in further detail.

Politics: A presidential election often stirs emotions regarding potential effects on the economy. Investors grow anxious about how a new president can influence market returns. It's Congress, however, that establishes tax laws and passes spending bills. Yet the president can indirectly affect the economy and the stock market in various ways such as the appointment of policymakers, development of international relations, and influential sway on new legislation.

Taxes: An example of a president's influence can be cited in signature legislation passed during Donald Trump's presidency, the Tax Cuts and Jobs Act of 2017. However, our tax system remains progressive, so the more you earn, the higher the tax rate within each tax bracket of subsequently higher income. A thorough understanding of tax regulations can be crucial. A financial professional can help identify potential issues a tax professional can help solve.

Inflation: Government spending, which most recently spiked with relief packages designed to assist U.S. citizens during the COVID-19 pandemic, can fuel concerns of inflationary hikes stemming from an influx of money thrust at the same consumer goods. A retiree's income can be impacted by the effect inflation can have on a fixed budget. The value of currency decreases because inflation erodes purchasing power.

Health pandemic: The coronavirus outbreak could impact how Americans view risks and re-examine healthy habits. That, potentially, could be one of the effects of COVID-19 as we assess how long a pandemic can last and if others will occur in our lifetimes. The cost of health care can be surprising throughout retirement. It could become an issue people focus on even more following the pandemic, which had a particularly acute impact on some U.S. elder care facilities.

Cybersecurity: Think you'll give up your smartphone in retirement? No way, right? It's here to stay, along with other intellectual gadgetry, including devices that have not been patented or invented. Retirees are becoming more tech-savvy, yet they can also be more trusting, which can be problematic when responding to potential scammers by phone, text, or email. Cybercrime often uses technology to target potential victims. Scammers, much like technology, figure to only grow more sophisticated over time.

CHAPTER 1

Longevity

You would think the prospect of the grave would loom more frightening as we age, yet many retirees say their number one concern is actually running out of money in their twilight years.[1] This concern is, unfortunately, justified, in part, because of one significant factor: We're living longer.

According to the Social Security Administration's 2011 Trustee Report, in 1950, the average life expectancy for a sixty-five-year-old man was seventy-eight, and the average for a sixty-five-year-old woman was eighty-one. In the 2022 Trustees Report issued by the SSA, those averages were 81.94 and 84.66, respectively.[2]

The bottom line of many retirees' budget woes comes down to this: They just didn't plan to live so long. Now, when we are younger and in our working years, that's not something we necessarily see as a bad thing; don't some people fantasize about living forever or, at least, reaching the ripe old age of one hundred?

However, with a longer lifespan, as we near retirement, we face a few snags. Our resources are finite—we only have so much money to provide income—but our lifespans can be

---

[1] Liz Weston. nerdwallet.com. March 25, 2021. "Will You Really Run Out of Money in Retirement?"
https://www.nerdwallet.com/article/finance/will-you-really-run-out-of-money-in-retirement
[2] Social Security Administration. 2023 Trustees Report. "Actuarial Life Table" https://www.ssa.gov/oact/STATS/table4c6.html

unpredictably long, perhaps longer than our resources allow. Also, longer lives don't necessarily equate with healthier lives. The longer you live, the more money you will likely need to spend on health care, even excluding long-term care needs like nursing homes.

You will also run into inflation. If you don't plan to live another twenty-five years but end up doing so, inflation at an average 3 percent will approximately double the price of goods over that time period. Put a harsh twist on that and the buying power of a ninety-year-old will be half of what they possessed if they retired at sixty-five.[3]

Because we don't necessarily get to have our cake and eat it, too, our collective increased longevity hasn't necessarily increased the healthy years of our lives. Typically, our life-extending care most widely applies to the time in our lives where we will need more care in general. Think of common situations like a pacemaker at eighty-five, or cancer treatment at seventy-eight.

"Wow, Matt," I can hear you say. "Way to start with the good news first."

I know, I've painted a grim picture, but all I'm concerned about here is cost. It's hard to put a dollar sign on life, but that is essentially what we're talking about when discussing longevity and finances. Living longer isn't a bad thing; it just costs more, and one key to a sound retirement strategy is preparing for it in advance.

I can give you a perfect example. I met one of my very first clients—we'll call her Jane— over twenty years ago. I had just graduated from college with a degree in finance and was getting my financial planning career underway. On the other hand, Jane was getting ready to retire after thirty-five years at one of our local banks. She had filled many positions at the bank during her career, acquiring a wealth of knowledge about

---

[3] Bob Sullivan, Benjamin Curry. Forbes. April 28, 2021. "Inflation And Retirement Investments: What You Need to Know."
https://www.forbes.com/advisor/retirement/inflation-retirement-investments/

finances, which she shared with the community by teaching financial literacy courses for free at her church. Jane and I share the same philosophy that if you know something that could potentially help others, you should share that information.

When Jane first came to see me, she said, "I'm not interested in working with a financial advisor close to my age because I imagine they will be retiring just like I am. I'm looking for someone young who can see me through my full retirement."

I appreciated her direct approach.

Jane's retirement income would come from her Social Security benefit, a modest pension, and supplemental income from her portfolio from the previous twenty years. Jane never had children of her own, so one of her goals was to be philanthropic during her life. She also wanted to set things up so that when she did pass away, most of her money would go to a handful of her favorite nonprofits.

Working together, Jane and I created a plan that allowed her to accomplish these goals, but only after the most crucial goal was taken care of—ensuring her income needs were met. Once that was done, she could feel comfortable enough to start giving annually to her favorite charities: her church, her local YMCA where she made many lifelong friends, and the animal shelter.

When she first retired, Jane had only planned to live until age eighty-five and figured that was a stretch. Today, Jane is in her late eighties, still enjoying decent health, a sharp mind, and a comfortable retirement. The Pension Protection Act of 2006 established qualified charitable distributions (QCDs). Once Jane was over seventy-and-a-half, we could use some of her tax-deferred IRA to continue her annual donations without increasing her taxable income. Better yet, these QCDs helped her satisfy the required minimum distribution (RMD) the IRS mandates she take out of her IRA every year.

Living longer may be more expensive, but it can be so meaningful when you plan for your "just-in-cases."

Retiring Early

A key part of planning for retirement revolves around retirement income. After all, retirement is cutting the cord that tethers you to your employer—and your monthly check. However, that check often comes with many other benefits, particularly health care. Health care is often the thing that can unexpectedly put dreams for an early retirement on hold. Some employers offer health benefits to their retired workers, but that number has declined drastically over the past several decades. In 1988, among employers who offered health benefits to their workers, 66 percent offered health benefits to their retirees. In 2022, that number was 21 percent.[4]

So, with employer-offered retirement health benefits on the wane, this becomes a major point of concern for anyone who is looking to retire, particularly those who are looking to retire before age sixty-five, when they would become eligible for Medicare coverage. Fidelity estimates that the average retired couple at age sixty-five will need approximately $315,000 for health care expenses in retirement, not including long-term care.[5] Do you think it's likely that cost will decrease?

Even if you are working until age sixty-five or have plans to cover your health expenses until that point, I often have clients who incorrectly assume Medicare is their golden ticket to cover all expenses. That is simply not the case.

---

[4] Henry J. Kaiser Family Foundation. October 27, 2022. "2022 Employer Health Benefits Survey Section Eleven: Retiree Health Benefits." https://www.kff.org/report-section/ehbs-2022-section-11-retiree-health-benefits/

[5] Fidelity Viewpoints. Fidelity. August 29, 2022.. "How to Plan for Rising Health Care Costs." https://www.fidelity.com/viewpoints/personal-finance/plan-for-rising-health-care-costs

Retiring Later

Planning for a long life in retirement partly depends on when you retire. While many people end up retiring earlier than they anticipated—due to injuries, layoffs, family crises, and other unforeseen circumstances—continuing to work past age sixty (and even sixty-five) is still a viable option for others and can be an excellent way to help establish financial comfort in retirement.

There are many reasons for this. For one, you obviously still earn a paycheck and the benefits accompanying it. Medical coverage and beefing up your retirement accounts with further savings can be significant by themselves but continuing your income also should keep you from dipping into your retirement funds, further allowing them the opportunity to grow.

Additionally, for many workers, their nine-to-five job is more than just clocking in and out. Having a sense of purpose can keep us active physically, mentally, and socially. That kind of activity and level of engagement may also help stave off many of the health problems that plague retirees. Avoiding a sedentary life is one of the advantages of staying plugged into the workforce, if possible.

The decisions we are sometimes forced to make are not always black and white. That was the case for my clients Ben and Anne, who had dreams of retiring in their early sixties; however, life unfolded in a way they could not have predicted.

In her early fifties, Anne was diagnosed with terminal cancer. She was forced to go on disability for a time while Ben kept working, primarily to retain health insurance for their family. Over the next few years, as Anne's health declined, Ben was forced to take more and more time away from work to care for her. Ultimately, he retired early so he could be there for her and their family. Tragically, Anne passed away four years after her diagnosis. Ben was left alone without his best friend and life partner to pick up the pieces, emotionally and financially.

One hard truth Ben had to face was that he likely did not have enough assets to sustain a comfortable retirement in the lifestyle he and Anne had before her diagnosis. As we worked together on his retirement income planning, we could only comfortably show his funds lasting until age eighty. The problem (and blessing) was that Ben was in excellent health, and his parents were both still alive in their nineties. Once Anne left her job due to her illness, she no longer carried life insurance outside of what she previously had through her employer. Due to her diagnosis, she could not obtain life insurance on her own. One saving grace for Ben was that he and Anne had diligently paid off their mortgage just a few years before her illness. Ben couldn't imagine leaving the home where he had so many good memories of raising their family. Thanks to this, I worked with Ben to explore an outside-the-box possibility.

I asked if he knew anything about reverse mortgages. At first, he was hesitant, but I explained the option that might be available to him after age sixty-two. With a reverse mortgage line of credit, he could access some of the equity from his home to help provide additional income without having a mandatory monthly mortgage payment.

We coordinated this strategy with his retirement income plan, and he was then able to have a conservative retirement income where his portfolio assets lasted beyond age ninety. He was so relieved to learn he had options other than returning to work full-time for several more years. He was open to working again but didn't want to be backed into a corner.

Health Care

Take a second to reflect on your health care plan. Although working up to or even past age sixty-five would allow you to avoid a coverage gap between your working years and Medicare, that may not be an option for you. Even if it is, when you retire, you will need to make some decisions about what kind of insurance coverage you may need to supplement your Medicare. Are there any medical needs you have that may require coverage in addition to Medicare? Did your parents or grandparents have any inherited medical conditions you might consider using a special savings plan to cover?

These are all questions that are important to review with your financial professional so you can be sure you have enough money put aside for health care.

Long-Term Care

Longevity means the need for long-term care is statistically more likely to happen. If you intend to pass on a legacy, planning for long-term care is paramount, since most estimates project nearly 70 percent of Americans will need some type of it.[6] However, this may be one of the biggest, most stressful pieces of longevity planning I encounter in my work. For one thing, who wants to talk about the point in their lives when they may feel the most limited? Who wants to dwell on what will happen if they no longer can toilet, bathe, dress, or feed themselves?

I get it; this is a less-than-fun part of planning. But a little bit of preparation now can go a long way!

When it comes to your longevity, just like with your goals, one of the important things to do is sit and dream. It may not be the fun, road-trip-to-the-Grand-Canyon kind of dreaming, but you can spend time envisioning how you want your twilight years to look.

For instance, if it is important for you to live in your home for as long as possible, who will provide for the day-to-day fixes and to-dos of housework if you become ill? Will you set aside money for a service, or do you have relatives or friends nearby whom you could comfortably allow to help you? Do you prefer in-home care over a nursing home or assisted living? This could

[6] Richard W. Johnson. urban.org. June 24, 2021. "What is the Lifetime Risk of Needing and Receiving Long-Term Services and Supports?" https://www.urban.org/research/publication/what-lifetime-risk-needing-and-receiving-long-term-services-and-supports

be a good time to discuss the possibility of moving into a retirement community versus staying where you are or whether it's worth moving to another state and leaving relatives behind.

These are all important factors to discuss with your spouse and children, as *now* is the right time to address questions and concerns. For instance, is aging in place more important to one spouse than the other? Are the friends or relatives who live nearby emotionally, physically, and financially capable of helping you for a time if you face an illness?

Many families I meet with find these conversations very uncomfortable, particularly when children discuss nursing home care with their parents. A knee-jerk reaction for many is to promise they will care for their aging parents. This is noble and well-intentioned, but there needs to be an element of realism here. Does "help" from an adult child mean they stop by and help you with laundry, cooking, home maintenance, and bills? Or does it mean they move you into their spare room when you have hip surgery? Are they prepared to help you use the restroom and bathe if that becomes difficult for you to do on your own?

I don't mean to discourage families from caring for their own; this can be a profoundly admirable relationship when it works out. However, I've seen families put off planning for late-in-life care based on a tenuous promise that the adult children would care for their parents, only to watch as the support system crumbles. Sometimes this is because the assumed caregiver hasn't given serious thought to the preparation they would need, both in a formal sense and regarding their personal physical, emotional, and financial commitments. This is often also because we can't see the future: Alzheimer's disease and other maladies of old age can exact a heavy toll. When a loved one reaches the point where he or she is at risk of wandering away or needs help with two or more activities of daily living, it can be more than one person or family can realistically handle.

If you know what you want, communicate with your family about both the best-case and worst-case scenarios. Then, hope for the best, and plan for the worst.

Realistic Cost of Care

Wrapped up in your planning should be a consideration for the cost of long-term care. The potential costs for such care and treatment can be underestimated, especially by those who have maintained robust health and find it difficult to envision future declines to their condition.

Another piece of planning for long-term care costs is anticipating inflation. It's common knowledge that prices have been and keep rising, which will lower your purchasing power on everything from food to medical care. Long-term care is a big piece of the inflation-disparity pie.

While local costs vary from state to state, following is the national median for various forms of long-term care (plus projections that account for a 3 percent annual inflation, so you can see what I am referencing):[7]

---

[7] Genworth Financial. June 2022. "Cost of Care Survey 2022." https://www.genworth.com/aging-and-you/finances/cost-of-care.html

Long-Term Care Costs: Inflation				
	Home Health Care, Homemaker Services	Adult Day Care	Assisted Living	Nursing Home (semi-private room)
Annual 2021	$59,488	$20,280	$54,000	$94,900
Annual 2031	$79,947	$27,255	$72,571	$127,538
Annual 2041	$107,442	$36,628	$97,530	$171,400
Annual 2051	$144,393	$49,225	$131,072	$230,347

Fund Your Long-Term Care

One of the mistakes I see are those who haven't planned for long-term care because they assume the government will provide everything. But that's a big misconception. The government has two health insurance programs: Medicare and Medicaid. These can greatly assist you in your health care needs in retirement but usually don't provide enough coverage to cover all your health care costs in retirement. My firm isn't a government outpost, so we don't get to make decisions when it comes to forming policy and specifics about either one of these programs. I'm going to give an overview of both, but if you want to dive into the details of these programs, you can visit www.Medicare.gov and www.Medicaid.gov.

Medicare
Medicare covers those aged sixty-five and older and those who are disabled. Medicare's coverage of any nursing-home-related health issues is limited. It might cover your nursing home stay

if it is not a "custodial" stay, and it isn't long-term. For example, if you break a bone or suffer a stroke, stay in a nursing home for rehabilitative care, and then return home, Medicare may cover you. But, if you have developed dementia or are looking to move to a nursing facility because you can no longer bathe, dress, toilet, feed yourself, or take care of your hygiene, etc., then Medicare is not going to pay for your nursing home costs.[8]

You can enroll in Medicare anytime during the three months before and three months after your sixty-fifth birthday. Miss your enrollment deadline, and you could risk paying increased premiums for the rest of your life.[9] On top of prompt enrollment, there are a few other things to think about when it comes to Medicare, not least among them being the need to understand the different "parts," what they do, and what they don't cover.

Part A

Medicare Part A is what you might think of as "classic" Medicare. Hospital care, some types of home health care, and major medical care fall under this. While most enrollees pay nothing for this service (as they likely paid into the system for at least ten years), you may end up paying, either based on work history or delayed signup. In 2023, the highest premium is $506 per month, and a hospital stay does have a deductible, $1,600.[10] And, if you have a hospital stay that surpasses sixty days, you could be looking at additional costs; keep in mind, Medicare doesn't pay for long-term care and services.

---

[8] Medicare.gov. "What Part A covers." https://www.medicare.gov/what-medicare-covers/part-a/what-part-a-covers.html
[9] Medicare.gov. "When can I sign up for Medicare?" https://www.medicare.gov/basics/get-started-with-medicare/sign-up/when-can-i-sign-up-for-medicare
[10] Medicare. "Medicare 2023 Costs at a Glance." https://www.medicare.gov/your-medicare-costs/medicare-costs-at-a-glance

Part B

Medicare Part B is an essential piece of wrap-around coverage for Medicare Part A. It helps pay for doctor visits and outpatient services. This also comes with a price tag: Although the Part B deductible is only $226 in 2023, you will still pay 20 percent of all costs after that, with no limit on out-of-pocket expenses. The Part B monthly premium for 2023 ranges from the standard amount of $164.90 to $560.50.[11]

Part C

Medicare Part C, more commonly known as Medicare Advantage plans, are an alternative to a combination of Parts A, B, and sometimes D. Administered through private insurance companies, these have a variety of costs and restrictions, and they are subject to the specific policies and rules of the issuing carrier.

Part D

Medicare Part D is also through a private insurer and is supplemental to Parts A and B, as its primary purpose is to cover prescription drugs. Like any private insurance plan, Part D has its quirks and rules that vary from insurer to insurer.

The Donut Hole
Even with a "Part D" in place, you may still have a coverage gap between what your Part D private drug insurance pays for your prescription and what basic Medicare pays. In 2023, the coverage gap is $4,660, meaning, after you meet your private prescription insurance limit, you will spend no more than 25

---

[11] Ibid.

percent of your drug costs out-of-pocket before Medicare will kick in to pay for more prescription drugs.[12]

Medicare Supplements

Medicare Supplement Insurance, MedSupp, Medigap, or plans labeled Medicare Part F, G, H, I, J . . . Known by a variety of monikers, this is just a fancy way of saying "medical coverage for those over sixty-five that picks up the tab for whatever the federal Medicare program(s) doesn't." Again, costs, limitations, etc., vary by carrier.

Does that sound like a bunch of government alphabet soup to you? It certainly does to me. And, did you read the fine print? Unpredictable costs, varied restrictions, difficult-to-compare benefits, donut holes, and coverage gaps. That's par for the course with health care plans through the course of our adult lives. What gives? I thought Medicare was supposed to be easier, comprehensive, and at no cost!

The truth is there is probably no stage of life when health care is easy to understand.

Consider Jeff, a former Director of IT for a major corporation. He was fortunate to be able to retire at the early age of sixty-two. Three years later, at age sixty-five, he signed up for Medicare. Jeff is a highly educated and proficient person, but even for him, trying to understand the ins and outs of Medicare was like trying to solve a Rubik's Cube.

In my hometown of Jackson, Michigan, we are fortunate to have a free local resource for retirees called the Department on Aging. I had Jeff set a meeting to go through his individual Medicare options. They were able to break down his options so he could understand and choose solutions that worked best for his situation. He was incredibly grateful that this community resource was available to him. I know it may not be the same in

---

[12] Medicare. "Costs in the coverage gap."
https://www.medicare.gov/drug-coverage-part-d/costs-for-medicare-drug-coverage/costs-in-the-coverage-gap

every community. Jackson is lucky to have this service. I know hundreds of retirees who have benefited from its resources and recommend it to everyone in our community.

It's worth doing an online search for similar resources in your community. You may be shocked at what is available!

The best thing you can do for yourself is to scope out the health care field early, compare costs often, and prepare for out-of-pocket costs well in advance—decades, if possible.

Medicaid

Medicaid is a program the states administer, so funding, protocol, and limitations vary. Compared to Medicare, Medicaid more widely covers nursing home care, but it targets a different demographic: those with low incomes.

If you have more assets than the Medicaid limit in your state and need nursing home care, you will need to use those assets to pay for your care. You will also have a list of additional state-approved ways to spend some of these assets over the Medicaid limit, such as pre-purchasing burial plots and funeral expenses or paying off debts. After that, your remaining assets fund your nursing home stay until they are gone, at which point Medicaid will jump in.

Some people aren't stymied by this, thinking they will just pass on their financial assets early, gifting them to relatives, friends, and causes so they can qualify for Medicaid when they need it. However, to prevent this exact scenario, Uncle Sam has implemented the look-back period. Currently, if you enroll in Medicaid, you are subject to having the government scrutinize the last five years of your finances for large gifts or expenses that may subject you to penalties, temporarily making you ineligible for Medicaid coverage.

So, if you're planning to preserve your money for future generations and retain control of your financial resources during your lifetime, you'll probably want to prepare for the costs of longevity beyond a "government plan."

Self-Funding

One way to fund a longer life is the old-fashioned way, through self-funding. There are a variety of financial tools you can use, and they all have their pros and cons. If your assets are in low-interest financial vehicles (savings, bonds, CDs), you risk letting inflation erode the value of your dollar. Or, if you are relying on the stock market, you have more growth potential, but you'll also want to consider the possible implications of market volatility. What if your assets take a hit? If you suffer a loss in your retirement portfolio in early or mid-retirement, you might have the option to "tighten your belt," so to speak, and cut back on discretionary spending to allow your portfolio the room to bounce back. But, if you are retired and depend on income from a stock account that just hit a downward stride, what are you going to do?

HSAs

These days, you might also be able to self-fund through a health savings account, or HSA, if you have access to one through a high-deductible health plan (you will not qualify to save in an HSA after enrolling in Medicare). In an HSA, any growth of your tax-deductible contributions will be tax-free, and any distributions paid out for qualified health costs are also tax-free. Long-term care expenses count as health costs, so, if this is an option available to you, it is one way to use the tax advantages to self-fund your longevity. Bear in mind, if you are younger than sixty-five, any money you use for nonqualified expenses will be subject to taxes and penalties, and, if you are older than sixty-five, any HSA money you use for non-medical expenses is subject to income tax.

LTCI

One slightly more nuanced way to pay for longevity, specifically for long-term care, is long-term care insurance, or LTCI. As car insurance protects your assets in case of a car accident and home insurance protects your assets in case something happens to your house, long-term care insurance aims to protect your assets in case you need long-term care in an at-home or nursing home situation.

As with other types of insurance, you will pay a monthly or annual premium in exchange for an insurance company paying for long-term care down the road. Typically, policies cover two to three years of care, which is adequate for an "average" situation: it's estimated 70 percent of Americans will need about three years of long-term care of some kind.

Now, there are a few oft-cited components of LTCI that make it unattractive for some:

- Expense—LTCI can be expensive. It is generally less expensive the younger you are, but a sixty-five-year-old couple who purchased LTCI in 2022 could expect to pay a combined amount of $3,750 each year for an average three-year coverage policy. And the annual cost only increases from there the older you are.[13]

- Limited options—Let's face it: LTCI may be expensive for consumers, but it can also be expensive for companies that offer it. With fewer companies willing to take on that expense, this narrows the market, meaning opportunities to price shop for policies with different options or custom benefits are limited.

- If you know you need it, you might not be able to get it— Insurance companies offering LTCI are taking on a risk that you may need LTCI. That risk is the foundation of the product—you may or may not need it. If you know you will need it because you have a dementia diagnosis or another illness for which you will need long-term care, you will likely not qualify for LTCI coverage.

---

[13] American Association for Long-Term Care Insurance. 2023. . "Long-Term Care Insurance Facts – Data – Statistics – 2022 Reports" https://www.aaltci.org/long-term-care-insurance/learning-center/ltcfacts-2022.php#2022costs-65

- Use it or lose it—If you have LTCI and are in the minority of Americans who die having never needed long-term care, all the money you paid into your LTCI policy is gone.
- Possibly fluctuating rates—Your rate is not locked in on LTCI. Companies maintain the ability to raise or lower your premium amounts. This means some seniors face an ultimatum: Keep funding a policy at what might be a less affordable rate *or* lose coverage and let go of all the money they paid in so far.

After that, you might be thinking, "How can people possibly be interested in LTCI?" But let me repeat myself—as many as 70 percent of Americans will need long-term care. And, although only one in ten Americans age fifty-five-plus have purchased LTCI, keep in mind the high cost of nursing home care. Can you afford $7,000 a month to put into nursing home care and still have enough left over to protect your legacy? This is a very real concern considering one set of statistics reported a two-in-three chance that a senior citizen will become physically or cognitively impaired in their lifetime.[14] So, not to sound like a broken record, but it is vitally important to have a plan in place to deal with longevity and long-term care if you intend to leave a financial legacy.

A few relevant statistics to keep in mind:

- The longer you live, the more likely you are to continue living; the longer you live, the more health care you will likely need to pay for.
- The average cost of a private nursing home room in the United States in 2021 was $9,034 a month.[15] But keep in mind, that is just the nursing home—it doesn't include

---

[14] payingforseniorcare.com. 2022. "Long-Term Senior Care Statistics" https://www.payingforseniorcare.com/statistics

[15] Genworth Financial. January 31, 2022. "Genworth 2020 Cost of Care Survey." https://www.genworth.com/aging-and-you/finances/cost-of-care.html

other medical costs, let alone pleasantries, like entertainment or hobby spending.

- In 2022, Fidelity calculated that a healthy couple retiring at age sixty-five could expect to pay around $315,000 over the course of retirement to cover health and medical expenses.

I know. "Whoa, there, Matt, I was hoping to have a realistic idea of health costs, not be driven over by a cement mixer!"

The good news is, while we don't know these exact costs in advance, we know there *will* be costs. And you won't have to pay your total Medicare lifetime premiums in one day as a lump sum. Now that you have a good idea of health care costs in retirement, you can *plan* for them! That's the real point, here: Planning in advance can keep you from feeling nickel-and-dimed to your wits' end. Instead, having a sizeable portion of your assets earmarked for health care can allow you the freedom to choose health care networks, coverage options, and long-term care possibilities you like and that you think offer you the best in life.

Product Riders

LTCI and self-funding are not the only ways to plan for the expenses of longevity. Some companies are getting creative with their products, particularly insurance companies. One way they are retooling to meet people's needs is through optional product riders on annuities and life insurance. Elsewhere in this book, I talk about annuity basics, but here's a brief overview: Annuities are insurance contracts. You pay the insurance company a premium, either as a lump sum or as a series of payments over a set amount of time, in exchange for guaranteed income payments. One of the advantages of an annuity is it has access to riders, which allow you to tweak your contract for a fee, usually about 1 percent of the contract value annually. One annuity rider some companies offer is a long-term care rider. If you have an annuity with a long-term care rider and are not in need of long-term care, your contract behaves as any annuity contract would—nothing changes. Generally speaking, if you reach a point when you can't perform multiple functions of daily life on your own, you notify the insurance company, and a representative will turn on those provisions of your contract.

Like LTCI, different companies and products offer different options. Some annuity long-term care riders offer coverage of two years in a nursing home situation. Others cap expenses at two times the original annuity's value. It greatly depends. Some people prefer this option because there isn't a "use-it-or-lose-it" piece; if you die without ever having needed long-term care, you still will have had the income benefit from the base contract. Still, as with any annuities or insurance contracts, there are the usual restrictions and limitations. Withdrawing money from the contract will affect future income payments, early distributions can result in a penalty, income taxes may apply, and, because the insurance company's solvency is what guarantees your payments, it's important to do your research about the insurance company you are considering purchasing a contract from.

Understandably, a discussion on long-term care is bound to feel at least a little tedious. Yet, this is an important piece of planning for income in retirement, particularly if you want to leave a legacy.

Unfortunately, I've seen too many people bury their heads in the sand, hoping and praying they will not face the hardships of long-term care and chronic illness later in life. By doing so, they have decided to self-fund their care should they ever need it. Maybe you have been blessed with significant financial resources and can confidently self-fund. If so, that's great! However, that is not an option for most. The financial statistics are scary, especially for a married couple. What happens when one spouse becomes chronically ill while the other remains a picture of great health (recall Ben and Anne's story)? Both spouses must have financial resources independent of the other.

Let's look at a hypothetical couple, Adam and Beth. For the last five years, Adam has been showing early signs of dementia and is ultimately diagnosed with primary progressive aphasia, a form of dementia that does not get better. He can't live on his own, and his wife, Beth, is becoming mentally burned out from acting as his primary caregiver. She starts to feel lonely and isolated while doing her best to care for her husband. Fortunately, she is able to hire two friends to help out part-time so she can run errands, go shopping, and go to her exercise classes. Eventually, Adam can no longer hold a conversation or even recognize his children.

Years earlier, while they were both still in excellent health, Adam and Beth had purchased long-term care policies at their own expense through their former employer. Unfortunately, the annual cost of the policy had increased so much that they ended up canceling both policies.

An option at this point if Adam were healthy would be a hybrid life insurance policy with living benefits. Unfortunately, with Adam diagnosed as needing LTC, the option Beth would have faced would be to self-fund care for Adam, drawing from their retirement nest egg. This would significantly drain their savings, and when Adam eventually passed away, Beth would still need income to supplement her Social Security benefit.

Not everyone will face chronic illness, but everyone will die someday. What if you could access some of that death benefit while still alive to help cover medical costs? And if you never need it, the life insurance policy pays a tax-free death benefit to your beneficiary—in this case, Beth. This would allow her to replenish assets spent to help cover Adam's care. Ultimately, Beth was able to set up these life insurance policies prior to Adam's diagnosis, and now she has a backup option to help her financially if she needs to use them during Adam's life.

Spousal Planning

Here's one thing to keep in mind no matter how you plan to save: Many of us will be planning for more than ourselves. Look back at all the stats on health events and the likelihood of long life and long-term care. If they hold true for a single individual, then the likelihood of having a costly health or long-term care event is even higher for a married couple. You'll be planning for not just one life, but two. So, when it comes to long-term care insurance, annuities, self-funding, or whatever strategy you are looking at using, be sure you are funding longevity for the both of you.

CHAPTER 2

Taxes

Where to begin with taxes? Perhaps by acknowledging we all bear responsibility for the resources we share. Roads, bridges, schools . . . it is the patriotic duty of every American to pay their fair share of taxes. Many would agree with me. However, while they don't mind paying their fair share, they're not interested in paying one cent more than that!

Now, just talking taxes probably takes your mind to April—tax season. You are probably thinking about all the forms you collect and how you file. Perhaps you are thinking about your certified public accountant or another qualified tax professional and saying to yourself, "I've already got taxes taken care of, thanks!"

However, what I see when people come into my office is that their relationship with their tax professional is purely a January through April relationship. That means they may have a tax professional, but not a tax *planner*.

What I mean is tax planning extends beyond filing taxes. In April, we are required to settle our accounts with the IRS to make sure we have paid up on our bill or to even the score if we have overpaid. But real tax planning is about making each financial move in a way that allows you to keep the most money in your pocket and out of Uncle Sam's.

Now, as a caveat, I want to emphasize I am neither a CPA nor a tax planner, but I see the way taxes affect my clients, and I have plenty of experience helping clients implement tax-efficient strategies in their retirement plans in conjunction with their tax professionals.

Tax planning is crucial to any retirement income plan, and I believe every advisor should be well-versed in this topic. As I noted earlier, I have a lot of knowledge about taxes; however, my team and I are not tax experts. We work extensively with our clients and their tax professionals to uncover every tax opportunity.

CPA Ed Slott is one of the country's foremost experts regarding retirement tax law and IRAs. He and his company are the nation's leading source for accurate, timely IRA expertise and analysis for financial advisors, institutions, consumers, and media. As an educational company, they work to:

- Train financial professionals to become knowledgeable, recognized leaders in the retirement marketplace
- Answer retirement savers' most important questions to continually provide practical, applicable, and easy-to-understand information on IRA, retirement, tax, and financial planning topics

I have been an Ed Slott Master Elite Advisor since 2006, and we require all advisors on our team to be part of Ed's elite advisory group. We also use tax planning software as a backdrop for helping guide clients in asking the right tax and income questions for their particular situation.

At Richmond Brothers, we believe in growth and continuous learning; this is just one way we walk the walk with our clients.

It is especially important to me to help my clients develop tax-efficient strategies in their retirement plans because each dollar they can keep is a dollar we can put to work.

Taxes are the *biggest* silent partner in most Americans' retirement plans. Why? Because they have spent thirty-plus years contributing to a tax-deferred 401(k) or 403(b). That was great each year when you received the deduction against your income for contributing to your own savings plan. The problem is that now you've accumulated $1 million or more in a tax-infested retirement account. Yes, tax-infested.

That $1 million does not all belong to you. Every dollar you withdraw from your plan is taxed as regular income. Let that sink in for a minute. So, while that $1 million looks good on paper, guess who also thinks it looks good? Uncle Sam.

The Fed

Now, in the United States, taxes can be a rather uncertain proposition. Depending on who is in the White House and which party controls Congress, we might be tempted to assume tax rates could either decline or increase in the next four to eight years accordingly. However, there is one (large!) factor we, as a nation, must confront: the national debt.

Currently, according to USDebtClock.org, we are over $31,000,000,000,000 in debt and climbing. That's $31 *trillion* with a "T." With just $1 trillion, you could park it in the bank at a zero percent interest rate and spend more than $54 million every day for fifty years without hitting a zero balance.

Even if Congress got a handle and stopped that debt from its daily compound, divided by each taxpayer, we each would owe about $246,000. So, will that be check, cash, or Venmo?[16]

My point here isn't to give you anxiety. I'm just cautioning you that even with the rosiest of outlooks on our personal income tax rates, none of us should count on low tax rates for the long term. Instead, you and your network of professionals (tax, legal, and financial) should constantly be looking for ways to take advantage of tax-saving opportunities as they come. After all, the best "luck" is when proper planning meets opportunity.

So, how can we get started?

---

[16] usdebtclock.org.

Know Your Limits

One of the foundational pieces of tax planning is knowing what tax bracket you are in, based on your income after subtracting pre-tax or untaxed assets. Your income taxes are based on your taxable income.

One reason to know your taxable income and your income tax rate is so you can see how far away you are from the next lower or higher tax bracket. This is particularly important when it comes to decisions such as gifting and Roth IRA rollovers.

For instance, when confronting the 2022 federal income tax return they filed in 2023, Mallory and Ralph's taxable income is just over $345,000, putting them in the 32 percent tax bracket and about $4,900 above the upper end of the 24 percent tax bracket. They have already maxed out their retirement funds' tax-exempt contributions for the year. Their daughter, Gloria, is a sophomore in college. This couple could shave a considerable amount off their tax bill if they use the $4,900 to help Gloria out with groceries and school—something they were likely to do, anyway, but now can deliberately be put to work for them in their overall financial strategy.

Now, I use Mallory and Ralph only as an example—your circumstances are probably different—but I think this nicely illustrates the way planning ahead for taxes can save you money.

Assuming a Lower Tax Rate

Many people anticipate being in a lower tax bracket in retirement. It makes sense: You won't be contributing to retirement funds; you'll be drawing from them. And you won't have all those work expenses—work clothes, transportation, lunch meetings, etc.

Yet, do you really plan on changing your lifestyle after retirement? Do you plan to cut down on the number of times you eat out, scale back vacations, and skimp on travel?

What I see in my office is many couples spend more in the first few years, or maybe the first decade, of retirement. Sure, that may taper off later on, but usually only just in time for their budget to be hit with greater health and long-term care expenses. Do you see where this is going? Many people plan as though their taxable income will be lower in retirement and are surprised when the tax bills come in and look more or less the same as they used to. It's better to plan for the worst and hope for the best, wouldn't you agree?

401(k)/IRA

One sometimes-unexpected piece of tax planning in retirement concerns your 401(k) or IRA. Most of us have one of these accounts or an equivalent. Throughout our working lives, we pay in, dutifully socking away a portion of our earnings in these tax-deferred accounts. There's the rub: tax-deferred. Not tax-free. Very rarely is anything free of taxation when you get down to it. Using 401(k)s and IRAs in retirement is no different. The taxes the government deferred when you were in your working years are now coming due, and you will pay taxes on that income at whatever your current tax rate is.

Just to ensure Uncle Sam gets his due, the government also has a required minimum distribution, or RMD, rule. Beginning at age seventy-three, you are required to withdraw a certain minimum amount every year from your 401(k) or IRA, or else you will face a tax penalty on any RMD monies you should have withdrawn but didn't—and that's on top of income tax. The SECURE Act 2.0 reduced the penalty to 25 percent (from 50 percent). Timely corrections also can reduce the penalty to 10 percent.[17]

---

[17] Jim Probasco. Investopedia.com. January 6, 2023. "SECURE 2.0 Act of 2022." https://www.investopedia.com/secure-2-0-definition-5225115

Of course, there is also the Roth account. You can think of the difference between a Roth and a traditional retirement account as the difference between taxing the seed and taxing the harvest. Because Roths are funded with post-tax dollars, there aren't tax penalties for early withdrawals of the principal nor are there taxes on the growth after you reach age fifty-nine-and-one-half. Perhaps best of all, there are no RMDs. Of course, you must own a Roth account for a minimum of five years before you are able to take advantage of all its features.

This is one more area where it pays to be aware of your tax bracket. Some people may find it advantageous to "convert" their traditional retirement account funds to Roth account funds in a year during which they are in a lower tax bracket. Others may opt to put any excess RMDs from their traditional retirement accounts into other products, like stocks or insurance.

Does that make your head spin? Understandable. That's why it's so important to work with a financial professional and tax planner who can help you execute these sorts of tax-efficient strategies and help you understand what you are doing and why.

Working with a financial professional who will look at your retirement assets and help you craft a plan to address some of the tax consequences—even if that plan is implemented over the next ten years—is vital. We help our clients by creating an income plan based on their net (after-tax) target monthly income needs.

For example, if you received two paychecks per month while working and, after deductions and taxes, your take-home pay was $3,000 per paycheck, you had $6,000 in net income per month. You used this money to buy gas and groceries and make your car and mortgage payments. As long as you didn't get to retirement carrying significant personal debt, you lived within your means, and $6,000 net income per month is a good place to start the retirement income planning process.

When I met with Sandra and James, they were embarrassed about the personal debt they had accumulated as they got closer and closer to their hopeful retirement ages. They were completely honest, sharing their outstanding credit card balances, interest rates, monthly payments, and what they owed on their cars and home. They were nervous that if they carried this debt into retirement, they might not be able to have the carefree lifestyle they dreamed of.

One huge saving grace for this couple was that although they had this debt, they also had diligently saved for retirement and accumulated just over $1.5 million in their 401(k) accounts. Additionally, much of their debt resulted from medical expenses above and beyond what their health insurance covered. Luckily, James survived his health scare, but now they were faced with medical bills that made them feel like they were drowning financially.

Immediately, my wheels were spinning on how to help them move toward their goals. Since they were both over fifty-nine-and-a-half, I knew they had an option inside their 401(k) distribution. Together, we created a plan for taking annual one-time taxable distributions out of their 401(k) to pay off all their debt, except for their mortgage. That added up to about $150,000 net, meaning we needed to withdraw a little over $200,000 total (taxes!) to pay off the debt.

Over the period leading up to age sixty-two, we freed up monthly debt payments of just over $2,500 a month. Sure, this lowered their total retirement asset base, but we were able to help them transition to retirement at sixty-two without the worry of massive debt hanging over their heads.

CHAPTER 3

Market Volatility

U p and down. Roller coaster. Merry-go-round. Bulls and bears. Peak-to-trough.

Sound familiar? This is the language we use to talk about the stock market. With volatility and spikes, even our language is jarring, bracing, and vivid.

Still, financial strategies tend to revolve around market-based products, for good reasons. For one thing, there is no other financial class that packs the same potential for growth, pound for pound, as stock-based products. Because of growth potential, inflation challenges, and new opportunities, it may be unwise to avoid the market entirely.

However, along with the potential for growth is the potential for loss. At the time this book was written, many of the people I've seen in my office came in feeling uneasy because of the economic fallout of the COVID-19 outbreak of 2020, followed by the economic downturn, and the inflation spike that happened in 2022.

So how do we balance these factors? How do we try to satisfy both the need for protection and the need for growth?

For one thing, it is important to recognize the value of diversity. Now, I'm not just talking about the diversity of assets among different kinds of stocks, or even different kinds of stocks and bonds. That's only one kind of diversity; while important, both stocks and bonds, though different, are both still market-based products. Most market-based products, even within a diverse portfolio, tend to rise or lower as a whole, just like an incoming tide. Therefore, a portfolio diverse in only market-sourced products won't automatically protect your assets during times when the market declines.

In addition to the sort of "horizontal diversity" you have by purchasing a variety of stocks and bonds from different companies, I also suggest you think about "vertical diversity," or diversity among asset classes. This means having different product types, including securities products, bank products, and insurance products—with varying levels of growth potential, liquidity, and protection—all in accordance with your unique situation, goals, and needs.

> *"Everyone has a plan until they get punched in the face." – Mike Tyson*

Time *in* the market is more important than *timing* the market. This statement is so simple and powerful; you see it in news headlines every time the stock market corrects or goes south—yet so many people ignore it.

When it comes to risk tolerance and retirement income planning, there is one truth you must acknowledge. You are now entering the distribution phase of your life, and *everything* is different compared to when you were in the accumulation phase. You now depend on your portfolio to help create an income stream that you hopefully don't outlive.

I see risk tolerance as more about your ability to answer this one question: How much downside are you willing to accept in your portfolio if the economy or markets don't behave nicely?

If you have $1 million and the economy goes into recession causing the markets to drop 30 percent, could you handle your $1 million shrinking to $700,000? I'm not suggesting you would like it, but can you tolerate it? Would that blow up your long-term retirement income plan? You must consider these questions when addressing downside or risk tolerance in retirement.

The Color of Money

When you're looking at the overall diversity of your portfolio, part of the equation is knowing which products fit in what category: what has liquidity, what has protection, and what has growth potential.

Before we dive in, keep in mind these aren't absolutes. You might think of liquidity, growth, and protection as primary colors. While some products will look pretty much yellow, red, or blue, others will have a mix of characteristics, making them more green, orange, or purple.

Growth

I like to think of the growth category as red. It's powerful, it's somewhat volatile, and it's also the category where we have the greatest opportunities for growth and loss. Often, products in the growth category will have a good deal of liquidity but very little protection. These are our market-based products and strategies, and we think of them mostly in shades of red and orange, to designate their growth and liquidity. This is a good place to be when you're young—think fast cars and flashy leather jackets—but its allure often wanes as you move closer to retirement. Examples of "red" products include:

- Stocks
- Equities
- Exchange-traded funds
- Mutual funds
- Corporate bonds
- Real estate investment trusts
- Speculations
- Alternative investments

Liquidity

Yellow is my liquid category color. I typically recommend having at least enough yellow money to cover six months' to a year's worth of expenses in case of emergency. Yellow assets don't need a lot of growth potential; they just need to be readily available when we need them. The "yellow" category includes assets like:

- Cash
- Money market accounts

Protection

The color of protection, to me, is blue, which can incorporate products such as annuities. Tranquil, peaceful, sure, even if it lacks a certain amount of flash. This is the direction I like to see people generally move toward as they're nearing retirement. The red, flashy look of stock market returns and the risk of possible overnight losses is less attractive as we near retirement and look for more consistency and reliability. While this category doesn't come with a lot of liquidity, the products here are backed by an insurance company, a bank, or a government entity. "Blue" products include things such as:

- Certificates of deposit (backed by banks)
- Government-based bonds (backed by the U.S. government)
- Life insurance (backed by insurance companies)
- Annuities (backed by insurance companies)

I believe in the markets; I believe in American business, and I believe that businesses will always innovate and evolve. Given this thought process, I believe that retirees should have market exposure. The question is, how much and where do you take this risk? Does your plan and your allocation have a fallback if you retire and the economy goes into recession for the next three years?

These are essential questions to ask *and* understand before taking that leap from working and collecting a paycheck to retiring and depending on your assets to provide an income stream.

401(k)s

I want to take a second to specifically address a product many retirees will be using to build their retirement income: the 401(k) and other retirement accounts. Any of these retirement accounts (IRAs, 401(k)s, 403(b)s, etc.) are basically "tax wrappers." What do I mean by that? Well, depending on your plan provider, a 401(k) could include target-date funds, passively managed products, stocks, bonds, mutual funds, or even variable, fixed, and fixed index annuities, all collected in one place and governed by rules (a.k.a. the "tax wrapper"). These rules govern how much money you can put inside, what ways you can put it in, when you will pay taxes on it, and when you can take the money out. Inside the 401(k), each of the products inside the "tax wrapper" might have its own fees or commissions, in addition to the management fee you pay on the 401(k) itself.

Now, fees can be troublesome. You can't get something for nothing, and fees are how many financial companies and professionals make a living. Yet, it's important to recognize even a fee with a fraction of a percentage point is money out of your pocket—money that represents not just the one-time fee of today but also represents an opportunity cost. A $100,000 IRA that earns 6 percent over a twenty-five-year period without investment fees would earn $430,000. But if just a 0.5 percent fee got factored into that investment, the IRA would be worth $379,000 in twenty-five years, a $50,500 decrease.[18] For someone close to retirement, how much do you think fees may have cost over their lifetime?

---

[18] Pam Krueger. Kiplinger.com. January 8, 2021. "How to Spot (and Squash) Nasty Fees That Hide in Your Investments" https://www.kiplinger.com/retirement/retirement-planning/602043/how-to-spot-and-squash-nasty-fees-that-hide-in-your

Even for those close to retirement, it's important to look at management fees and assess if you think you're getting what you pay for. Over the course of ten years, those costs can add up, and you may have decades ahead of you in which you will need to rely on your assets. Bottom line, be informed and ask questions. There is nothing wrong with being informed about what fees you pay or learning the value you may get for the fees you incur.

Dollar-Cost Averaging

With 401(k)s and other market-based retirement products, dollar-cost averaging is a concept that can work in your favor when you are investing for the long term. When the market is trending up, if you are consistently paying in money, month over month, great; your investments can grow, and you are adding to your assets. When the market takes a dip, no problem; your dollars buy more shares at a lower price. At some point, we hope the market will rebound, in which case your shares can grow and possibly be more valuable than they were before. This concept is what we call "dollar-cost averaging." While it can't ensure a profit or guarantee against losses, it's a time-tested strategy for investing in a volatile market.

However, when you are in retirement, this strategy may work against you. You may have heard of "reverse" dollar-cost averaging. Before, when the market lost ground, you were "bargain-shopping"; your dollars purchased more assets at a reduced price. When you are in retirement, you are no longer the purchaser; you are selling. So, in a down market, you have to sell more assets to make the same amount of money as what you made in a favorable market.

A fallback for some advisors is to tell clients that, historically, the market will bounce back while attempting to ease investors' concerns.

There's some basis for this thinking; thus far, the market has always rebounded to loftier heights than before. But this is no guarantee, and the prospect of potentially higher returns in five years may not be very helpful in retirement if you are relying on the income from those returns to pay this month's electric bill, for example.

At Richmond Brothers, we use tools designed to help our clients understand how we can aid them in planning for market volatility. As an independent firm, we have investment options that can partially or (in some cases) completely mitigate downside. We craft plans that can ride through recessions and even mitigate against sequence of return risk.

You and I have no way of knowing the future. That's why we say to hope for the best but plan for the worst. We create plans that allow you to financially live through the downturns that inevitably will happen several times throughout your twenty, thirty, or forty-year retirement.

To simplify things for clients, we created our own series of scores we call the Retire Confident Navigator scores. Each of these can help address your concerns and questions about market volatility.

Is There a "Perfect" Product?

To bring us back around to the discussion of protection, growth, and liquidity, the ideal product would be a "ten" in all three categories, right? Completely guaranteed, doubling in size every few years, and accessible whenever you want. Does such a product exist? Absolutely not.

Instead of running in circles looking for that perfect product, the silver bullet, the unicorn of financial strategies, it's more important to circle back to the concept of a balanced, asset-diverse portfolio.

This is why it could be prudent to work with a knowledgeable financial professional who knows what various financial products can do and how to use them in your personal retirement strategy.

CHAPTER 4

Retirement Income

etirement. For many of us, it's what we've saved for and dreamed of, pinning our hopes to a magical someday. Is that someday full of traveling? Is it filled with grandkids? Gardening? Maybe your fondest dream is simply never having to work again, never having to clock in or be accountable to someone else.

Your ability to do these things all hinges on *income*. Without the money to support these dreams, even a basic level of work-free lifestyle is unsustainable. That's why planning for your income in retirement is so foundational. But where do we begin?

It's easy to feel overwhelmed by this question. Some may feel the urge to amass a large lump sum and then try to put it all in one product—insurance, investments, liquid assets—to provide all the growth, liquidity, and income they need. Instead, I think you need a more balanced approach. After all, retirement planning isn't magic. Like I mention elsewhere, there is no single product that can be all things to all people (or even all things to one person). No approach works unilaterally for everyone. That's why it's important to talk to a financial professional who can help you lay down the basics and take you step-by-step through the process. Not only will you have the assurance you have addressed the areas you need to, but you will also have an ally who can help you break down the process and help keep you from feeling overwhelmed.

Sources of Income

Thinking of all the pieces of your retirement expenses might be intimidating. But, like cleaning out a junk drawer or revisiting that garage remodel, once you have laid everything out, you can begin to sort things into categories.

Once you have a good overall picture of where your expenses will lie, you can start stacking up the resources to cover them.

Social Security

Social Security is a guaranteed, inflation-protected federal insurance program playing a significant part in most of our retirement plans. From delaying until you've reached full retirement age or beyond to examining spousal benefits, as I discuss elsewhere in this book, there is plenty you can do to try to make the most of this monthly benefit. As with all your retirement income sources, it's important to consider how to make this resource stretch to provide the most bang and buck for your situation.

Pension

Another generally reliable source of retirement income for you might be a pension, if you are one of the lucky people who still has one.

If you don't have a pension, go ahead and skim on to the next section. If you do have a pension, keep on reading.

Because your pension can be such a central piece of your retirement income plan, you will want to put some thought into answering basic questions about it.

How well is your pension funded? Since the heyday of the pension plan, companies and governments have neglected to fund their pension obligations, causing a persistent problem with this otherwise reliable asset.

Consider the factors at play, though. Pensions had been underfunded and gained a boost from strong market performance in 2021. What happens to the solvency of those pension funds if the market declines?

It can be worthwhile to keep tabs on your pension's health and know what your options are for withdrawing your pension. If you have already retired and made those decisions, this may be a foregone conclusion. If not, it pays to know what you can expect and what decisions you can make, such as taking spousal options to cover your husband or wife if he or she outlives you.

Also, some companies are incentivizing lump-sum payouts of pensions to reduce the companies' payment liabilities. If that's the case with your employer, talk to your financial professional to see if it might be prudent to do something like that or if it might be better to stick with lifetime payments or other options.

Your 401(k) and IRA

One "modern way" to save for retirement is in a 401(k) or IRA (or their nonprofit or governmental equivalents). These tax-advantaged accounts are, in my opinion, a poor substitute for pensions, but one of the biggest disservices we do to ourselves is to not take full advantage of them in the first place. According to one article, only 41 percent of Americans invest in a 401(k), though 68 percent of employed Americans have access to a 401(k) benefit option.[19]

Also, if you have changed jobs over the years, do the work of tracking down any benefits from your past employers. You might have an IRA here or a 401(k) there; keep track of those so you can pull them together and look at those assets when you're ready to look at establishing sources of retirement income.

---

[19] Amin Dabit. personalcapital.com. April 1, 2021. "The Average 401k Balance by Age." https://www.personalcapital.com/blog/retirement-planning/average-401k-balance-age/

Do You Have...

- Life insurance?
- Annuities?
- Long-term care insurance?
- Any passive income sources?
- Stock and bond portfolios?
- Liquid assets? (What's in your bank account?)
- Alternative investments?
- Rental properties?

If you are going through the work of sitting with a financial professional, it's important to look at your full retirement income picture and pull together *all* your assets, no matter how big or small. From the free insurance policy offered at your bank to the sizable investment in your brother-in-law's modestly successful furniture store, you want to have a good idea of where your money is.

Retirement Income Needs

How much income will you need in retirement? How do you determine that? A lot of people work toward a random number, thinking, "If I can just have a million dollars, I'll be comfortable in retirement!" Don't get me wrong; it is possible to save up a lot of money and then retire in the hopes you can keep your monthly expenses lower than some set estimation. But I think this carries a general risk of running out of money. Instead, I work with my clients to find out what their current and projected income needs are and then work from there to see how we might cover any gaps between what they have and what they want.

Goals and Dreams

I like to start with your pie in the sky. Do you find yourself planning for your vacations more thoroughly than you do your retirement? Maybe it's because planning a vacation is less stressful: Having a week at the beach go awry is, well, a walk on the beach compared to running out of money in retirement. Whatever the case, perhaps it would be better if you thought of your retirement as a vacation in and of itself—no clocking in, no boss, no overtime. If you felt unlimited by financial strain, what would you do?

Would an endless vacation for you mean Paris and Rome? Would it mean mentoring at children's clubs or serving at the local soup kitchen? Or maybe it would mean deepening your ties to those immediately around you—neighbors, friends, and family. Maybe it would mean more time to take part in the hobbies and activities you love. Have you been considering a second (or even third) act as a small-business owner, turning a hobby or passion into a revenue source?

This is your time to daydream and answer the question: If you could do anything, what would you do?

After that, it's a matter of putting a dollar amount on it. What arc the costs of round-the-world travel? One couple I know said their highest priority in retirement was being able to take each of their grandchildren on a cross-country vacation every year. That's a pretty specific goal—one that is reasonably easy to nail down a budget for.

Current Budget

Compiling a current expense report is one of the trickiest pieces of retirement preparation. Many people assume the expenses of their lives in retirement will be different—lower. After all, there will be no drive to work, no need for a formal wardrobe, and, perhaps most impactful of all, no more saving for retirement!

Yet, we often underestimate our daily spending habits. That's why I typically ask my clients to bring in their bank statements for the past year—they are reflective of your *actual* spending, not just what you think you're spending.

I can't count the number of times I have sat with a couple, asked them about their spending, and heard them throw out a number that seemed incredibly low. When I ask them where the number came from, they usually say they estimated based on their total bills. Yet, our spending is so much more than our mortgage, utilities, cable, phone, car, grocery, or credit card bills.

"What about clothes?" I ask, "Or dining out? What about gifts and coffees and last-minute birthday cards?" That's when the lights come on.

This is why I suggest collecting a year's worth of information. There is usually no such thing as a one-time purchase. Did you buy new furniture? Even if that is a rarity, do you think that will be the last time you *ever* buy furniture?

Another hefty expense is spending on the kids. Many of the couples I work with are quick to help their adult children, whether it's something like letting them live in the basement, paying for college, babysitting, paying an occasional bill, or contributing to a grandchild's college fund. Research concluded that 22 percent of adults receive some kind of financial support from parents. That segment jumps to almost 30 percent when factoring the generation we call millennials.[20]

My clients sometimes protest that what they do for their grown children can stop in retirement. They don't *need* to help. But I get it. Parents like to feel needed. And, while you never want to neglect saving for retirement in favor of taking on financial risks (like your child's student debt), the parents who help their adult children do so in part because it helps them feel fulfilled.

---

[20] Kamaron McNair. magnifymoney.com. October 26, 2021. "Nearly 30% of Millenials Still Receive Financial Support From Their Parents" https://www.magnifymoney.com/blog/news/parental-financial-support-survey/

When it comes down to expenses, including (and especially) spending on your family, don't make your initial calculations based on what you *could* whittle your budget down to if you *had* to. Instead, start from where you are. Who wants to live off a bare-bones bank account in retirement?

Other Expenses

Once you have nailed down your current budget and your dreams or goals for retirement, there are a few other outstanding pieces to think about—some expenses many people don't take the time to consider before making and executing a plan. But I'm assuming you want to get it right, so let's take a look.

Housing

Do you know where you want to live in retirement? This makes up a substantial piece of your income puzzle—since the typical American household owns a home, and it's generally their largest asset.

Some people prefer to live right where they are for as long as they can. Others have been waiting for retirement to pull the trigger on an ambitious move, like purchasing a new house, or even downsizing. Whatever your plans and whatever your reasons, there are quite a few things to consider.

Mortgage
Do you still have a mortgage? What may have been a nice tax boon in your working years could turn into a financial burden in your retirement. After all, when you are on a limited income, a mortgage is just one more bill sapping your financial strength. It is something to put some thought into, whether you plan to age in place or are considering moving to your dream home, buying a house out of state, or living in a retirement community.

Upkeep and Taxes

A house without a mortgage still requires annual taxes. While it's tempting to think of this as a once-a-year expense, when you have limited earning potential, your annual tax bill might be something into which you should put a little more forethought.

The costs of homeownership aren't just monetary. When you find yourself dealing with more house than you need, it can drain your time and energy. From keeping clutter at bay to keeping the lawn mower running, upkeep can be extensive and expensive. For some, that's a challenge they heartily accept and can comfortably take on. For others, the idea of yard work or cleaning an area larger than they need feels foolish.

For instance, Peggy discovered after her knee replacement that most of her house was inaccessible to her when she was laid up.

"It felt ridiculous to pay someone else to dust and vacuum a house I was only living in 40 percent of!"

Practicality and Adaptability

Erik and Magda are looking to retire within the next two decades. They just sold their old three-bedroom ranch-style house. Their twins are in high school, and the couple has wanted to "upgrade" for years. Now they live in a gorgeous 1940s three-story house with all the kitchen space they ever wanted, five sprawling bedrooms, and a library and media room for themselves and their children. Within months of moving in, the couple realized a house perfect for their active teens would no longer be perfect for them in five to fifteen years.

"We are paying the mortgage for this house, but we've started saving for the next one," said Magda, "because who wants to climb two flights of stairs to their bedroom when they're seventy-eight?"

Others I know have encountered a similar situation in their personal lives. After a health crisis, one couple found the luxurious tub for two they toiled to install had become a specter of a bad slip and a potential safety risk. It's important to think through what your physical reality could be. I always emphasize to my clients that they should plan for whatever their long-term future might hold, but it's amazing how many people don't give it much thought.

Contracts and Regulations

If you are looking into a cross-country move, be aware of new tax tables or local ordinances in the area where you are looking to move. After all, you don't want to experience sticker-shock when you are looking at downsizing or reducing your bills in retirement.

Along the same lines, if you are moving into a retirement community, be sure to look at the fine print. What happens if you must move into a different situation for long-term care? Will you be penalized? Will you be responsible for replacing your slot in the community? What are all the fees, and what do they cover?

Inflation

As I write this in 2023, America has experienced a wave of inflation following a lengthy period of low inflation. Inflation zoomed to 9.1 percent in June 2022, its highest mark since November 1981.[21]

Core inflation is yet another measurement that excludes goods with prices that tend to be more volatile, such as food and energy costs. Core inflation for a 12-month period ending in

---

[21] tradingeconomics.com. 2022 Data/2023 Forecast/1914-2021 Historical. "United States Inflation Rate" https://tradingeconomics.com/united-states/inflation-cpi

February 2023 was 5.5 percent. It so happened energy prices rose 5.2 percent over that timeframe.[22]

However, inflation isn't a one-time bump; it has a cumulative effect. Again, that can impact the price of groceries greater than other goods. Even with relatively low inflation over the past few decades, an item you bought in 1997 for two dollars will cost about $3.70 today.[23] Want to go to a show? A $20 ticket in 1997 would cost $43.01 in 2023[24]

What if, in retirement, we hit a stretch like the late seventies and early eighties, when annual inflation rates of 10 percent became the norm? It may be wise to consider some extra padding in your retirement income plan to account for any potential increase in inflation in the future.

Aging

Also, in the expense category, think about longevity. We all hope to age gracefully. However, it's important to face the prospect of aging with a sense of realism.

The elephant in the room for many families is long-term care. No one wants to admit they will likely need it, but estimates indicate almost 70 percent of us will.[25] Aging is a significant piece of retirement income planning because you'll want to figure out how to set aside money for your care, either at home or away from it. The more comfortable you get with discussing your wishes and plans with your loved ones, the easier planning for the financial side of it can be.

---

[22] U.S. Inflation Calculator. "United States Core Inflation Rates (1957-2022)" https://www.usinflationcalculator.com/inflation/united-states-core-inflation-rates/

[23] In2013dollars.com. "$2 in 1997 is worth $3.70 today" https://www.in2013dollars.com/us/inflation/1997?amount=2

[24] In2013dollars.com "Admission to movies, theaters, and concerts priced at $20 in 1997>$40.34 in 2022" https://www.in2013dollars.com/Admission-to-movies,-theaters,-and-concerts/price-inflation

[25] Moll Law Group. 2022. "The Cost of Long-Term Care." https://www.molllawgroup.com/the-cost-of-long-term-care.html

I denote health care and potential long-term care costs in more detail elsewhere in this book, but suffice it to say nursing home care tends to be very expensive and typically isn't something you get to choose when you will need.

It isn't just the costs of long-term care that pose a concern in living longer. It's also about covering the possible costs of everything else associated with living longer. For instance, if Henry retires from his job as a biochemical engineer at age sixty-five, perhaps he planned to have a very decent income for twenty years, until age eighty-five. But what if he lives until he's ninety-five? That's a whole third—ten years—more of personal income he will need.

Putting It All Together

Whew! So, you have pulled together what you have, and you have a pretty good idea of where you want to be. Now your financial professional and you can go about the work of arranging what assets you *have* to cover what you *need*—and how you might try to cover any gaps.

Like the proverbial man in the Bible who built his house on a rock, I like to help my clients figure out how to cover their day-to-day living expenses—their needs—with insurance and other guaranteed income sources like pensions and Social Security.

Again, you should keep in mind there isn't one single financial vehicle, asset, or source to fill all your needs, and that's okay. One of the challenges of planning for your income in retirement concerns figuring out what products and strategies to use. You can release some of that stress when you accept the fact you will probably need a diverse portfolio—potentially with bonds, stocks, insurance, and other income sources—not just one massive money pile.

One way to help shore up your income gaps is by working with your financial professional and a qualified tax advisor to mitigate your tax exposure. If you have a 401(k) or IRA, a tax advisor in your corner can help you figure out how and when to take distributions from your account in a way that doesn't push you into a higher tax bracket. Or you might learn how to use tax-advantaged bonds more effectively. Effective tax planning isn't necessarily about "adding" to your income. Especially regarding retirement, it's less about what you make than it is about what you keep. Paying a lower tax bill keeps more money in your pocket, which is where you want it when it comes to retirement income.

Now you can look at ways to cover your remaining retirement goals. Are there products like long-term care insurance specific to a certain kind of expense you anticipate? Is there a particular asset you want to use for your "play" money—money for trips and gifts for the grandkids? Is there any way you can portion off money for those charitable legacy plans?

Once you have analyzed your income wants, needs, and the assets to realistically cover them, you may have a gap. The masterstroke of a competent financial professional will be to help you figure out how you will cover that gap. Will you need to cut out a round of golf a week? Maybe skip the new car? Or will you need to take more substantial action?

One way to cover an income gap is to consider working longer or even part-time before retirement and even after that magical calendar date. This may not be the best "plan" for you; disabilities, work demands, and physical or emotional limitations can hinder the best-laid plans to continue working. However, if it is physically possible for you, this is one considerable way to help your assets last, for more than one reason.

In fact, 46 percent of the Americans responding to a survey report they plan to work part-time after retiring, while 18 percent indicated they planned to work past the age of seventy.[26]

When you're retired, you no longer have an employer paying you a steady check. It is up to you to make sure you have saved and planned for the income you need.

---

[26] Palash Ghosh. Forbes.com. May 6, 2021. "A Third Of Seniors Seek To Work Well Past Retirement Age, Or Won't Retire At All, Poll Finds" https://www.forbes.com/sites/palashghosh/2021/05/06/a-third-of-seniors-seek-to-work-well-past-retirement-age-or-wont-retire-at-all-poll-finds/?sh=1d2ece836b95

CHAPTER 5

Social Security

S ocial Security is often the foundation of retirement income. Backed by the strength of the U.S. Treasury, it provides perhaps the most dependable paycheck you will have in retirement.

From the time you collect your first paycheck from the job that made you a bonafide taxpayer (for me, it was when I was working as a line cook at a local diner not far from my home.), you are paying into the grand old Social Security system. What grew and developed out of the pressures of the Great Depression has become one of the most popular government programs in the country, and, if you pay in for the equivalent of ten years or more, you, too, can benefit from the Social Security program.

Now, before we get into the nitty-gritty of Social Security, I'd like to address a current concern: Will Social Security still be there for you when you reach retirement age?

The Future of Social Security

This question is ever-present as headlines trumpet an underfunded Social Security program, alongside the sea of baby boomers retiring in droves and the comparatively smaller pool of younger people who are funding the system.

The Social Security Administration itself acknowledges this concern as each Social Security statement now contains a link to its website (ssa.gov) and a page entitled, "Will Social Security Be There For Me?"

Just a reminder, as if you needed one, that nothing in life is guaranteed. Additionally, depending on who you're listening to, Social Security funds may run low before 2034 thanks to the financial instability and government spending that accompanied the 2020 COVID-19 pandemic.

Before you get too discouraged, though, here are a few thoughts to keep you going:

- Even if the program is only paying 78 cents on the dollar for scheduled benefits, 78 percent is notably not zero.
- The Social Security Administration has made changes in the distant and near past to protect the fund's solvency, including increasing retirement ages and striking certain filing strategies.
- There are many changes Congress could make, and lawmakers routinely discuss how to fix the system, such as further increasing full retirement age and eligibility.
- One thing no one is seriously discussing? Reneging on current obligations to retirees or the soon-to-retire.

Take heart. The real answer to the question, "Will Social Security be there for me?" is still yes.

This question is important to consider when you look at how much we, as a nation, rely on this program. Did you know Social Security benefits replace about 40 percent of a person's original income when they retire?[27]

If you ask me, that's a pretty significant piece of your retirement income puzzle.

Another caveat? You may not realize this, but no one can legally "advise" you about your Social Security benefits.

---

[27] ssa.gov. "Alternate Measure of Replacement Rates for Social Security Benefits and Retirement Income"
https://www.ssa.gov/policy/docs/ssb/v68n2/v68n2p1.html.

"But, Matt," you may be thinking, "isn't that part of what you do? And what about that nice gentleman at the Social Security Administration office I spoke with on the phone?"

Don't get me wrong. Social Security Administration employees know their stuff. They are trained to understand policies and programs, and they are usually pretty quick to tell you what you can and cannot do. But the government specifically stipulates, because Social Security is a benefit you alone have paid into and earned, your Social Security decisions, too, are yours alone.

When it comes to financial professionals, we can't push you in any direction, but—there's a big but here—working with a well-informed financial professional is still incredibly handy for your Social Security decisions. Why? Because someone who's worth his or her salt will know what withdrawal strategies might pertain to your specific situation and will ask questions that can help you determine what you are looking for when it comes to your Social Security.

For instance, some people want the highest possible monthly benefit. Others want to start their benefits early, not always because of financial need. I heard about one man who called in to start his Social Security payments the day he qualified, just because he liked to think of it as the government paying back a debt it owed him, and he enjoyed the feeling of receiving a check from Uncle Sam.

Whatever your reasons, questions, or feelings regarding Social Security, the decision is yours alone; but working with a financial professional can help you put your options in perspective by showing you—both with industry knowledge and with proprietary software or planning processes— where your benefits fit into your overall strategy for retirement income.

One reason the federal government doesn't allow for "advice" related to Social Security, I suspect, is so no one can profit from giving you advice related to your Social Security benefit—or from providing any clarifications. Again, this is a sign of a good financial professional. Those who are passionate about their work will be knowledgeable about what benefit strategies might be to your advantage and will happily share those possible options with you.

Full Retirement Age

When it comes to Social Security, it seems like many people only think so far as "yes." They don't take the time to understand the various options available. Instead, because it is common knowledge you can begin your benefits at age sixty-two, that's what many of us do. While more people are opting to delay taking benefits, age sixty-two is still firmly the most popular age to start.[28]

What many people fail to understand is, by starting benefits early, they may be leaving a lot of money on the table. You see, the Social Security Administration bases your monthly benefit on two factors: your earnings history and your full retirement age (FRA).

From your earnings history, they pull the thirty-five years you made the most money and use a mathematical indexing formula to figure out a monthly average from those years. If you paid into the system for less than thirty-five years, then every year you didn't pay in will be counted as a zero.

Once they have calculated what your monthly earning would be at FRA, the government then calculates what to put on your check based on how close you are to FRA. FRA was originally set at sixty-five, but, as the population aged and lifespans lengthened, the government shifted FRA later and later, based on an individual's year of birth. Check out the following chart to see when you will reach FRA.[29]

---

[28] Chris Kissell. moneytalknews.com. January 20, 2021. "This Is When the Most People Start Taking Social Security."
https://www.moneytalksnews.com/the-most-popular-age-for-claiming-social-security/
[29] Social Security Administration. "Full Retirement Age."
https://www.ssa.gov/planners/retire/retirechart.html

Age to Receive Full Social Security Benefits*	
(Called "full retirement age" [FRA] or "normal retirement age.")	
Year of Birth*	FRA
1937 or earlier	65
1938	65 and 2 months
1939	65 and 4 months
1940	65 and 6 months
1941	65 and 8 months
1942	65 and 10 months
1943-1954	66
1955	66 and 2 months
1956	66 and 4 months
1957	66 and 6 months
1958	66 and 8 months
1959	66 and 10 months
1960 and later	67
*If you were born on Jan. 1 of any year, you should refer to the previous year. (If you were born on the 1st of the month, we figure your benefit [and your full retirement age] as if your birthday was in the previous month.)	

When you reach FRA, you are eligible to receive 100 percent of whatever the Social Security Administration says is your full monthly benefit.

Starting at age sixty-two, for every year before FRA you claim benefits, your monthly check is reduced by 5 percent or more. Conversely, for every year you delay taking benefits past FRA, your monthly benefit increases by 8 percent (until age seventy—after that, there is no monetary advantage to delaying Social Security benefits). While your circumstances and needs may vary, a lot of financial professionals still urge people to at least consider delaying until they reach age seventy.

Why wait?[30]

Taking benefits early could affect your monthly check by _____.								
62	63	64	65	FRA 66	67	68	69	70
-25 %	-20 %	-13.3 %	-6.7 %	0	+8 %	+16 %	+24 %	+32 %

My Social Security

If you are over age thirty, you have probably received a notice from the Social Security Administration telling you to activate something called "My Social Security." This is a handy way to learn more about your particular benefit options, to keep track of what your earnings record looks like, and to calculate the benefits you have accrued over the years.

Essentially, My Social Security is an online account you can activate to see what your personal Social Security picture looks like, which you can do at www.ssa.gov/myaccount. This can be extremely helpful when it comes to planning for income in retirement and figuring up the difference between your anticipated income versus anticipated expenses.

---

[30] Social Security Administration. April 2021. "Can You Take Your Benefits Before Full Retirement Age?"
https://www.ssa.gov/planners/retire/applying2.html

COLA

Social Security is a largely guaranteed piece of the retirement puzzle: If you get a statement that reads you should expect $1,000 a month, you can be sure you will receive $1,000 a month. But there is one variable detail, and that is something called the cost-of-living adjustment, or COLA.

The COLA is an increase in your monthly check meant to address inflation in everyday life. After all, your expenses will likely continue to experience inflation in retirement, but you will no longer have the opportunity for raises, bonuses, or promotions you had when you were working. Instead, Social Security receives an annual cost-of-living increase tied to the Department of Labor's Consumer Price Index for Urban Wage Earners and Clerical Workers, or CPI-W. If the CPI-W measurement shows inflation rose a certain amount for regular goods and services, then Social Security recipients will see that reflected in their COLA.

COLA adjustments have climbed as high as 14.3 percent (1980) and in 2023 reached 8.7 percent, the largest increase in more than forty years. But in a no- or low-inflation environment, such as in 2010, 2011, and 2016, Social Security recipients will not receive an adjustment.[31] Some view the COLA as a perk, bump, or bonus, but, in reality, it works more like this: Your mom sends you to the store with $2.50 for a gallon of milk. Milk costs exactly $2.50. The next week, you go back with that same amount, but it is now $2.52 for a gallon, so you go back to Mom, and she gives you 2 cents. You aren't bringing home more milk—it just costs more money.

So the COLA is less about "making more money" and more about keeping seniors' purchasing power from eroding when inflation is a big factor, such as in 1975, when it was 8 percent![32] Still, don't let that detract from your enthusiasm about COLAs;

---

[31] ssa.gov. "Cost-Of-Living Adjustments" ssa.gov/oact/cola/colaseries.html
[32] Social Security Administration. "Cost-Of-Living Adjustment (COLA) Information for 2022." https://www.ssa.gov/cola/

after all, what if Mom's solution was: "Here's the same $2.50; try to find pennies from somewhere else to get that milk!"?

Spousal Benefits

We've talked about FRA, but another big Social Security decision involves spousal benefits.

If you or your spouse has a long stretch of zeros in your earnings history—perhaps if one of you stayed home for years, caring for children or sick relatives—you may want to consider filing for spousal benefits instead of filing on your own earnings history. A spousal benefit can be up to 50 percent of the primary wage earner's benefit at full retirement age.

To begin drawing a spousal benefit, you must be at least sixty-two years old, and the primary wage earner must have already filed for his or her benefit. While there are penalties for taking spousal benefits early, you cannot earn credits for delaying past full retirement age.[33]

Like I wrote, the spousal benefit can be a big deal for those who don't have a very long pay history, but it's important to weigh your own earned benefits against the option of withdrawing based on a fraction of your spouse's benefits.

To look at how this could play out, let's use a hypothetical couple: Mary Jane, who is sixty, and Peter, who is sixty-two.

Let's say Peter's benefit at FRA, in his case sixty-seven, would be $1,600. If Peter begins his benefits right now, four years before FRA, his monthly check will be $1,200. If Mary Jane begins taking spousal benefits in two years at the earliest date possible, her monthly benefits will be reduced by 67.5 percent, to $520 per month (remember, at FRA, the most she can qualify for is half of Peter's FRA benefit).

What if Peter and Mary Jane both wait until FRA? At sixty-seven, Peter begins taking his full benefit of $1,600 a month. Two years later, when she reaches age sixty-seven, Mary Jane

---

33 Social Security Administration. "Retirement Planner: Benefits For You As A Spouse." https://www.ssa.gov/planners/retire/applying6.html

will qualify for $800 a month. By waiting until FRA, the couple's monthly benefit goes from $1,720 to $2,400.

What if Peter delays until age seventy to get his maximum possible benefit? For each year past FRA he delays, his monthly benefits increase by 8 percent. This means, at seventy, he could file for a monthly benefit of $2,015. However, delayed retirement credits do not affect spousal benefits, so as soon as Peter files at seventy, Mary Jane would also file (at age sixty-eight) for her maximum benefit of $800, so their highest possible combined monthly check is $2,815.[34]

When it comes to your Social Security benefits, you obviously will want to consider whether a monthly check based on a fraction of your spouse's earnings will be comparable to or larger than your own earnings history.

Divorced Spouses

There are a few considerations for those of us who have gone through a divorce. If you 1) were married for ten years or more *and* 2) have since been divorced for at least two years *and* 3) are unmarried *and* 4) your ex-spouse qualifies to begin Social Security, you qualify for a spousal benefit based on your ex-husband or ex-wife's earnings history at FRA. A divorced spousal benefit is different from the married spousal benefit in one way: You don't have to wait for your ex-spouse to file before you can file yourself.[35]

For instance, Charles and Moira were married for fifteen years before their divorce, when he was thirty-six and she was forty. Moira has been remarried for twenty years, and, although Charles briefly remarried, his second marriage ended after a few years. Charles' benefits are largely calculated based on his

---

[34] Office of the Chief Actuary. Social Security Administration. "Social Security Benefits: Benefits for Spouses." https://www.ssa.gov/OACT/quickcalc/spouse.html#calculator

[35] Social Security Administration. "Retirement Planner: If You Are Divorced." https://www.ssa.gov/planners/retire/divspouse.html

many years of volunteering in schools, meaning his personal monthly benefit is close to zero.

Although Moira has deferred her retirement, opting to delay benefits until she is seventy, Charles can begin taking benefits calculated from Moira's work history at FRA as early as sixty-two. However, he will also have the option of waiting until FRA to collect the maximum, or 50 percent of Moira's earned monthly benefit at her FRA.

Widowed Spouses

If your marriage ended with the death of your spouse, you might claim a benefit for your spouse's earned income as his or her widow/widower, called a survivor's benefit. Unlike a spousal benefit or divorced benefits, if your husband or wife dies, you can claim his or her full benefit. Also, unlike spousal benefits, if you need to, you can begin taking income when you turn sixty. However, as with other benefit options, your monthly check will be permanently reduced for withdrawing benefits before FRA.

If your spouse began taking benefits before he or she died, you can't delay withdrawing your survivor's benefits to get delayed credits. The Social Security Administration maintains you can only get as much from a survivor's benefit as your deceased spouse might have received, had he or she lived.[36]

Taxes, Taxes, Taxes

With Social Security, as with everything, it is important to consider taxes. It may be surprising, but your Social Security benefits are not tax-free. Despite having been taxed to accrue those benefits in the first place, you may have to pay Uncle Sam income taxes on up to 85 percent of your Social Security.

---

[36] Social Security Administration. "Social Security Benefit Amounts For The Surviving Spouse By Year Of Birth."
https://www.ssa.gov/planners/survivors/survivorchartred.html

The Social Security Administration figures these taxes using what they call "the provisional income formula." Your provisional income formula differs from the adjusted gross income you use for your regular income taxes. Instead, to find out how much of your Social Security benefit is taxable, the Social Security Administration calculates it this way:

Provisional Income = Adjusted Gross Income + Nontaxable Interest + ½ of Social Security

See that piece about nontaxable interest? That generally means interest from government bonds and notes. It surprises many people that, although you may not pay taxes on those assets, their income will count against you when it comes to Social Security taxation.

Once you have figured out your provisional income (also called "combined income"), you can use the following chart to figure out your Social Security taxes.[37]

---

[37] Social Security Administration. "Benefits Planner: Income Taxes and Your Social Security Benefits." https://www.ssa.gov/planners/taxes.html

Taxes on Social Security		
Provisional Income = Adjusted Gross Income + Nontaxable Interest + ½ of Social Security		
If you are ____ and your provisional income is____, then...		Uncle Sam will tax ___ of your Social Security
Single	Married, filing jointly	
Less than $25,000	Less than $32,000	0%
$25,000 to $34,000	$32,000 to $44,000	Up to 50%
More than $34,000	More than $44,000	Up to 85%

This is one more reason it may benefit you to work with financial and tax professionals. They can look at your entire financial picture to make your overall retirement plan as tax-efficient as possible—including your Social Security benefit.

Working and Social Security: The Earnings Test

If you haven't reached FRA, but you started your Social Security benefits and are still working, things get a little hairy.

Because you have started Social Security payments, the Social Security Administration will pay out your benefits (at that reduced rate, of course, because you haven't reached your FRA). Yet, because you are working, the organization must also withhold from your check to add to your benefits, which you are already collecting. See how this complicates matters?

To address the situation, the government has what is called the earnings test. For 2023, you can earn up to $21,240 without it affecting your Social Security check if you're younger than full retirement age. But, for every $2 you earn past that amount, the Social Security Administration will withhold $1. The earnings test loosens in the year of your FRA; if you are reaching FRA in 2023, you can earn up to $56,520 before you run into the earnings test, and the government only withholds $1 for every $3 past that amount.

The month you reach FRA, you are no longer subject to any earnings withholding. For instance, if you are still working and will turn sixty-six on December 28, 2023, you would only have to worry about the earnings test until December, and then you can ignore it entirely. Keep in mind, the money the government withholds from your Social Security benefits while you are working before FRA will be tacked back onto your benefits check after FRA.[38]

Should I defer my Social Security until I'm older or take a reduced benefit now? The answer is not the same for everyone. If you're married, do you know the best way for the two of you to draw your Social Security benefits for your unique circumstances? Do you know that Social Security is not taxed the same as IRA or pension distributions in retirement? How does this affect your net monthly income goal? We help clients address these questions as they consider the best way to draw on their benefits.

For example, Nick and June are a married couple. June retired early and is about to turn sixty-two. Nick is still working but planning to retire when he turns sixty-six next year. They're wondering when they should start drawing on their Social Security benefits. Both are in decent health, but not a single person in June's family has lived beyond seventy-five. Nick's dad, however, is still alive and doing well at age eighty-six.

As part of Richmond Brothers' FearLess Financial Approach, we would complete an inventory of all retirement accounts and possible income streams for June and Nick's retirement. In doing so, we might discover they could live comfortably on

---

[38] Social Security Administration. "Receiving Benefits White Working" https://www.ssa.gov/benefits/retirement/planner/whileworking.html.

$7,500 per month net (after taxes). We know that once June turned sixty-two and Nick retired, they could both begin receiving Social Security as part of their retirement income, but let's take a step back and consider their options.

Let's say June's benefit at age sixty-two is $1,800 a month. Nick's benefit out to age seventy (maximum deferral age) ends up at just over $4,000 per month (remember your benefit grows by 8 percent per year for each year you defer beyond your FRA up to age seventy). In this case, I may recommend June start her benefit now while Nick delays until age seventy for the maximum benefit. This could help alleviate June's concern about family history and longevity. Plus, we could use their portfolio to take a higher income to fill the gap from Nick's retirement until age seventy. If Nick lives a long time like his dad, he has maxed out his Social Security benefit for the remainder of his life.

If Nick or June pre-deceases the other, the surviving spouse will get to keep the higher of the two monthly benefits but not both. In this scenario, Nick and June's portfolio will last even longer because, once Nick turns seventy, they will have a much lower need for supplemental income to achieve their $7,500 net monthly target.

Again, everyone's circumstances are different. How and when you draw your benefits should help you and your family achieve your goals. It doesn't matter what your friends or your golf buddies tell you. Find a solution that works for *you*.

CHAPTER 6

401(k)s & IRAs

Have you heard? Today's retirement is not your parents' retirement. You see, back in the day, it was pretty common to work for one company for the vast majority of your career and then retire with a gold watch and a pension.

The gold watch was a symbol of the quality time you had put in at that company, but the pension was more than a symbol. Instead, it was a guarantee—as solid as your employer—that they would repay your hard work with a certain amount of income in your old age. Did you see the caveat there? Your pension's guarantee was *as solid as your employer*. The problem was, what if your employer went under?

Companies that failed couldn't pay their retired employees' pensions, leading to financial challenges for many. Beginning in 1974 with Congress' passage of the Employee Retirement Income Security Act, federal legislation and regulations aimed at protecting retirees were everywhere. One piece of legislation included a relatively obscure section of the Internal Revenue Code, added in 1978. Section 401(k), to be specific.

IRC section 401, subsection k, created tax advantages for employer-sponsored financial products, even if the main contributor was the employee him or herself. Over the years, more employers took note, beginning an age of transition away from pensions and toward 401(k) plans. A 401(k) is a retirement account with certain tax benefits and restrictions on the investments or other financial products inside of it.

Essentially, 401(k)s and their individual retirement account (IRA) counterparts are "wrappers" that provide tax benefits around assets; typically, the assets that compose IRAs and 401(k)s are mutual funds, stock and bond mixes, and money market accounts. However, IRA and 401(k) contents are becoming more diverse these days, with some companies offering different kinds of annuity options within their plans.

Where pensions are defined-*benefit* plans, 401(k)s and IRAs are defined-*contribution* plans. The one-word change outlines the basic difference. Pensions spell out what you can expect to receive from the plan but not necessarily how much money it will take to fund those benefits. With 401(k)s, an employer sets a standard for how much they will contribute (if any), and you can be certain of what you are contributing. Still, there is no outline for what you can expect to receive in return for those contributions.

Modern employment looks very different. A 2022 survey by the Bureau of Labor Statistics determined U.S. workers stayed with their employers a median of 4.1 years. Workers ages fifty-five to sixty-four had a little more staying power and were most likely to stay with their employer for about ten years.[39] Participation in 401(k) plans has steadily risen this century, totaling $7.3 trillion in assets in 2021 compared to $3.1 trillion in 2011. The survey revealed about 60 million active participants engaged in 401(k) plans.[40]

Those statistics make it clear that 401(k) plans have replaced pensions at many companies and, for that matter, a gold watch.

---

[39] Bureau of Labor Statistics. September 22, 2022. "Employee Tenure Summary." https://www.bls.gov/news.release/tenure.nr0.htm

[40] Investment Company Institute. October 11, 2021. "Frequently Asked Questions About 401(k) Plan Research" https://www.ici.org/faqs/faq/401k/faqs_401k#:~:text=In%202020%2C%20there%20were%20about,of%20former%20employees%20and%20retirees.

If there is anything to learn from this paradigm shift, it's that you must look out for yourself. Whether you have worked for a company for two years or twenty, you are still the one who has to look out for your own best interests. That holds doubly true when it comes to preparing for retirement. If you are one of the lucky ones who still has a pension, good for you. But for the rest of us, it is likely a 401(k)—or possibly one of its nonprofit- or government-sector counterparts, a 403(b) or 457 plan—is one of your biggest assets for retirement.

Some employers offer incentives to contribute to their company plans, like a company match. On that subject, I have one thing to say: *Do it!* Nothing in life is free, as they say, but a company match on your retirement funds is about as close to free money as it gets. If you can make the minimum to qualify for your company's match at all, go for it.

Now, it's likely, during our working years, we mostly "set and forget" our 401(k) funding. Because it is tax-advantaged, your employer is taking money from your paycheck—before taxes— and putting it into your plan for you. Maybe you got to pick a selection of investments, or maybe your company only offers one choice of investment in your 401(k). Either way, while you are gainfully employed, your most impactful decision may just be the decision to continue funding your plan in the first place. But, when you are ready to retire or move jobs, you have choices to make requiring a little more thought and care.

When you are ready to part ways with your job, you have a few options:

- Leave the money where it is
- Take the cash (and pay income taxes and perhaps a 10 percent additional federal tax if you are younger than age fifty-nine-and-one-half)
- Transfer the money to another employer plan (if the new plan allows)
- Roll the money over into a self-directed IRA

Now, these are just general options. You will have to decide, hopefully with the help of a financial professional, what's right for you. For instance, 401(k)s are typically pretty closely tied to the companies offering them, so when changing jobs, it may not always be possible to transfer a 401(k) to another 401(k). Leaving the money where it is may also be out of the question—some companies have direct cash payout or rollover policies once someone is no longer employed.

Also, remember what we mentioned earlier about how we change jobs more often these days? That means you likely have a 401(k) with your current company, but you may also have a string of retirement accounts trailing you from other jobs.

When it comes to your retirement income, it's important to be able to pull together *all* your assets, so you can examine what you have and where, and then decide what you will do with it.

Tax-Qualified, Tax-Preferred, Tax-Deferred … Still TAXED

Financial media often cite IRAs and 401(k)s for their tax benefits. After all, with traditional plans, you put your money in, pre-tax, and it hopefully grows for years, even decades, untaxed. That's why these accounts are called "tax-qualified" or "tax-deferred" assets. They aren't *tax-free!* Rarely does Uncle Sam allow business to continue without receiving his piece of the pie, and your retirement assets are no different. If you didn't pay taxes on the front end, you will pay taxes on the money you withdraw from these accounts in retirement. Don't get me wrong: This isn't an inherently good or bad thing; it's just the way it is. It's important to understand, though, for the sake of planning ahead.

In retirement, many people assume they will be in a lower tax bracket. Are you planning to pare down your lifestyle in retirement? Perhaps you are, and perhaps you will have substantially less income in retirement. But many of my clients tell me they want to live life more or less the same as they always have. The money they would previously have spent on business attire or gas for their commute they now want to spend on hobbies and grandchildren. That's all fine, and for many of them, it is doable, but does it put them in a lower tax bracket? Probably not.

Keep in mind, IRAs, 401(k)s, and their alternatives have a few limitations because of their special tax status. For one thing, the IRS sets limits on your contributions to these retirement accounts. If you are contributing to a 401(k) or an equivalent nonprofit or government plan, your annual contribution limit is $22,500 (as of 2023). If you are fifty or older, the IRS allows additional contributions, called "catch-up contributions," of up to $7,500 on top of the regular limit of $22,500. For an IRA, the limit is $6,500, with a catch-up limit of an additional $1,000.[41] Beginning in 2026, catch-up contributions for individuals with income exceeding $145,000 must transfer into a Roth IRA.[42]

Because their tax advantages come from their intended use as retirement income, withdrawing funds from these accounts before you turn fifty-nine-and-one-half can carry stiff penalties. In addition to fees your investment management company might charge, you will have to pay income tax *and* a 10 percent federal tax penalty, with few exceptions.

The fifty-nine-and-one-half rule for retirement accounts is incredibly important to remember, especially when you're young. Younger workers are often tempted to cash out an IRA from a previous employer and then are surprised to find their checks missing 20 percent of the account value to income taxes, penalty taxes, and account fees.

Many millennials I see in my practice say, while they may be socking money away in their workplace retirement plan, it is

---

[41] IRS.gov. December 8, 2022. "401(k) limit increases to $22,500 for 2023, IRA limit rises to $6,500" https://www.irs.gov/newsroom/401k-limit-increases-to-22500-for-2023-ira-limit-rises-to-6500
[42] Robert Powell. thestreet.com. "Ask the Hammer: Catch-up Contributions Now Permitted Until 2026" https://www.thestreet.com/retirement-daily/ask-the-hammer/catch-up-contributions-now-permitted-until-2026

often the *only* place they are saving. This could be problematic later because of the fifty-nine-and-one-half rule; what if you have an emergency? It is important to fund your retirement, but you need to have some liquid assets handy as emergency funds. This can help you avoid breaking into your retirement accounts and incurring taxes and penalties because of the fifty-nine-and-one-half rule.

RMDs

Remember how we talked about the 401(k) or IRA being a "tax wrapper" for your funds? Well, eventually, Uncle Sam will want a bite of that candy bar. So, when you turn seventy-three, the government requires you withdraw a portion of your account, which the IRS calculates based on the size of your account and your estimated lifespan. This required minimum distribution, or RMD, is the government's insurance it will collect some taxes, at some point, from your earnings. Because you didn't pay taxes on the front end, you will now pay income taxes on whatever you withdraw, including your RMDs.

Let me reiterate something I pointed out in the Longevity chapter. Beginning at age seventy-three, you are required to withdraw a certain minimum amount every year from your 401(k) or IRA, or else you will face a tax penalty on any RMD monies you should have withdrawn but didn't—and that's on top of income tax. The SECURE Act 2.0 reduced the penalty to 25 percent (from 50 percent). Timely corrections also can reduce the penalty to 10 percent.[43]

Even after you begin RMDs, you can still also continue contributing to your 401(k) or IRAs if you are still employed, which can affect the whole discussion on RMDs and possible tax considerations. The SECURE Act 2.0 raised the RMD age to seventy-three from seventy-two. In addition, the latest

[43] Jim Probasco. Investopedia.com. January 6, 2023. "SECURE 2.0 Act of 2022." https://www.investopedia.com/secure-2-0-definition-5225115

legislation stipulates the RMD age will increase to seventy-five for those turning seventy-four after December 31, 2032.[44]

If you don't need income from your retirement accounts, RMDs can seem like more of a tax burden than an income boon. While some people prefer to reinvest their RMDs, this comes with the possibility of additional taxation: You'll pay income taxes on your RMDs and then potential capital gains taxes on the growth of your investments. If you are legacy-minded, there are other ways to use RMDs, many of which have tax benefits.

SECURE Act 2.0 provisions

In addition to changes imposed for RMD ages, Secure Act 2.0 also expanded access to retirement savings using different methods. Provisions in the legislation go into effect at different times, ranging from 2023-25.

- Beginning January 2, 2024, plan participants can access up to $1,000 (once a year) from retirement savings for emergency personal or family expenses without paying a 10 percent early withdrawal penalty.
- Beginning January 2, 2024, employees can establish a Roth emergency savings account of up to $2,500 per participant.
- Beginning January 2, 2024, domestic abuse survivors can withdraw the lesser of $10,000 or 50 percent of their retirement account without penalty.
- Beginning January 1, 2023, victims of a qualified, federally declared disaster can withdraw up to $22,000 from their retirement account without penalty.[45]

Permanent Life Insurance

One way to turn those pesky RMDs into a legacy is through permanent life insurance. Assuming you need the death benefit coverage and can qualify for it medically, if properly structured,

---

[44] Ibid.
[45] Betterment.com. January 12, 2023. "SECURE Act 2.0: Signed into Law" https://www.betterment.com/work/resources/secure-act-2

these products can pass on a sizeable death benefit to your beneficiaries, tax-free, as part of your general legacy plan.

ILIT

Another way to use RMDs toward your legacy is to work with an estate planning attorney to create an irrevocable life insurance trust (ILIT). This is basically a permanent life insurance policy placed within a trust. Because the trust is irrevocable, you would relinquish control of it, but, unlike with just a permanent life insurance policy, your death benefit won't count toward your taxable estate.

Annuities

Because annuities can be tax-deferred, using all or a portion of your RMDs to fund an annuity contract can be one way to further delay taxation while guaranteeing your income payments (either to you or your loved ones) later. Of course, this assumes you don't need the RMD income during your retirement.

Qualified Charitable Distributions

If you are charity-minded, you may use your RMDs toward a charitable organization instead of using them for income. You must do this directly from your retirement account (you can't take the RMD check and *then* pay the charity) for your withdrawals to be qualified charitable distributions (QCDs), but this is one way of realizing some of the benefits of a charitable legacy during your own lifetime. You will not need to pay taxes on your QCDs, and they won't count toward your annual charitable tax deduction limit, plus you'll be able to see how the organization you are supporting uses your donations. You should consult a financial professional on how to correctly make a QCD.

Roth IRA

Since the Taxpayer Relief Act of 1997, there has been a different kind of retirement account, or "tax wrapper," available to the public: the Roth. Roth IRAs and Roth 401(k)s each differ from their traditional counterparts in one big way: You pay your taxes on the front end. This means, once your post-tax money is in the Roth account, as long as you follow the rules and limitations of that account, your distributions are truly tax-free. You won't pay income tax when you take withdrawals, so, in turn, you don't have to worry about RMDs. However, Roth accounts have the same limitations as traditional 401(k)s and IRAs when it comes to withdrawing money before age fifty-nine-and-one-half, with the added stipulation that the account must have been open for at least five years in order for the account holder to make withdrawals.

People sometimes wonder if they can still invest in a Roth IRA or a Roth 401(k) when they are approaching retirement. To me, this is a sign that there is a lot of misunderstanding and possibly misinformation surrounding Roth accounts. Believe it or not, a Roth account is available in one form or another to almost every single retiree I have worked with, with very few exceptions. I hope you're interested in learning more about this type of account for your retirement planning. It does not matter whether you're fifty or seventy-five; the Roth is an option for you to consider.

Many work plans, such as a 401(k) or a 403(b), now offer Roth provisions where you can designate your employee contribution as a Roth 401(k) or Roth 403(b) contribution. You do not get to deduct your contribution as it goes into the plan, but the goal is to build a portion of your retirement assets in a future tax-free account like a Roth 401(k) or 403(b).

You can get funds into a Roth in two main ways: First, if you have earned income (i.e., work income), you may be eligible to contribute directly to a Roth IRA. In 2023, you would be eligible to contribute up to $6,500 dollars if you are under fifty and up to $7,500 if you are fifty or older in 2023. This is called a catch-up provision. However, the IRS does impose income limits on these contributions. This means you can earn too much to be eligible to make these contributions. It's worth noting that if your employer retirement plan (i.e., 401(k) or 403(b)) offers a Roth option, there are absolutely no income limitations to contribute to your workplace plan and use the Roth option.

What if you are already retired and do not have any work income? Option two is called a conversion, where you convert funds from an IRA account to a Roth IRA up to the balance of your IRA. If you have an IRA with $1 million, you are welcome to convert 100 percent of that account to your Roth IRA.

What's the downfall, you ask? Only convert what you can pay the tax bill on. In this example, you would owe income tax on all $1 million of the conversion in one tax year. That may be too much to deal with and may not even make sense. But it is an option for you to consider.

Many clients I have worked with over the years instead opt to act on partial IRA to Roth IRA conversions. They may convert $50,000 one year, $100,000 the next year, and slowly work through conversions over time to balance the tax liability. Additionally, when you turn sixty-three and every year after, you will want to pay attention to your taxable income for Medicare planning purposes. This is in addition to the federal and/or state income tax you may owe on these conversions.

Taking Charge

As mentioned earlier, the 401(k) and IRA have largely replaced pensions, but they aren't an equal trade.

Pensions are employer-funded; the money feeding into them is money that wouldn't ever show up on your pay stub. Because 401(k)s are self-funded, you must actively and consciously save. This distinction has made a difference when it comes to funding retirement. Fidelity Investments published a story detailing that the average 401(k) balance for a person age fifty-five to sixty-four is $189,800, but the median likely tells the full story. The median 401(k) balance for a person age fifty-five to sixty-four is \$56,450. Those figures reflect Fidelity accounts from the third quarter of 2022.[46]

There can be many reasons why people underfund their retirement plans, like being overwhelmed by the investment choices or taking withdrawals from IRAs when they leave an employer. Still, the reason at the top of the list is this: People simply aren't participating to begin with.

So, whether you use a 401(k) with an employer or an IRA alternative with a private company, separate from your workplace, the most important retirement savings decision you can make is to sock away your money somewhere in the first place.

---

[46] Arielle O'Shea. Nerd Wallet. December 22, 2022. "The Average 401(k) Balance by Age" https://www.nerdwallet.com/article/investing/the-average-401k-balance-by-age

CHAPTER 7

Annuities

In my practice, I offer my clients a variety of products—from securities to insurance—all designed to help them reach their financial goals. You may be wondering: Why single out a single product in this book?

Well, while most of my clients have a pretty good understanding of business and finance, I sometimes find those who have the impression there must be magic involved. Some people assume there is a magic finance wand we can wave to change years' worth of savings into a strategy for retirement income. But it's not as easy as a goose laying golden eggs or the Fairy Godmother turning a pumpkin into a coach!

Finances aren't magic; it takes lots of hard work and, typically, several financial products and strategies to pull together a complete retirement plan. Of all the financial products I work with, it seems people find none more mysterious than annuities. And, if I may say, even some of those who recognize the word "annuity" have a limited understanding of the product. So, in the interest of demystifying annuities, let me tell you a little about what an annuity is.

In general, insurance is a financial hedge against risk. Car owners buy auto insurance to protect their finances in case they injure someone or someone injures them. Homeowners have house insurance to protect their finances in case of a fire, flood, or another disaster. People have life insurance to protect their finances in case of untimely death. Almost juxtaposed to life

79

insurance, people have annuities in case of a long life; annuities can give you financial protection by providing consistent and reliable income payments.

The basic premise of an annuity is you, the annuitant, pay an insurance company some amount in exchange for their contractual guarantee they will pay you income for a certain time period. How that company pays you, for how long, and how much they offer are all determined by the annuity contract you enter into with the insurance company.

How You Get Paid

There are two ways for an annuity contract to provide income: The first is through what is called annuitization, and the second is through the use of income riders. We'll get into income riders in a bit, but let's talk about annuitization. That nice, long word is, in my opinion, one reason annuities have a reputation for mystery and misinformation.

Annuitization

When someone "annuitizes" a contract, it is the point where he or she turns on the income stream. Once a contract has been annuitized, there is no going back. With annuities, if the policyholder lives longer than the insurance company planned, the insurance company is still obligated to pay him or her, even if the payments end up being way more than the contract's actual value. If, however, the policyholder dies an untimely death, depending on the contract type, the insurance company may keep anything left of the money that funded the annuity— nothing would be paid out to the contract holder's survivors. You see where that could make some people balk? Now, modern annuities rarely rely on annuitization for the income portion of the contract, and instead have so many bells and whistles that the old concept of annuitization seems outdated, but because this is still an option, it's important to at least understand the basic concept.

Riders

Speaking of bells and whistles, let's talk about riders. Modern annuities have a lot of different options these days, many in the form of riders you can add to your contract for a fee—usually about 1 percent of the contract value per year. Each rider has its particulars, and the types of riders available will vary by the type of annuity contract purchased, but I'll just briefly outline some of these little extras:

- Lifetime income rider: Contract guarantees you an enhanced or flexible income for life
- Death benefit rider: Contract pays an enhanced death benefit to your beneficiaries even if you have annuitized
- Return of premium rider: Guarantees you (or your beneficiaries) will at least receive back the premium value of the annuity
- Long-term care rider: Provides a certain amount, sometimes as much as twice the normal income benefit amount for a period of time to help pay for long-term care if the contract holder is moved to a nursing home or assisted living situation

This isn't an extensive look, and usually the riders have fancier names based on the issuing company, like "Lorem Ipsum Insurance Company Income Preferred Bonus Fixed Index Annuity rider," but I just wanted to show you what some of the general options are in layperson's terms.

Types of Annuities

Annuities break down into four basic types: immediate, variable, fixed, and fixed index.

Immediate

Immediate annuities primarily rely on annuitization to provide income—you give the insurance company a lump sum up front, and your payments begin immediately. Once you begin receiving income payments, the transaction is irreversible, and you no longer have access to your money in a lump sum. When you die, any remaining contract value is typically forfeited to the insurance company.

All other annuity contract types are "deferred" contracts, meaning you fund your policy as a lump sum or over a period of years and you give it the opportunity to grow over time—sometimes years, sometimes decades.

Variable

A variable annuity is an insurance contract as well as an investment. It's sold by insurance companies, but only through someone who is registered to sell investment products. With a variable annuity contract, the insurance company invests your premiums in subaccounts that are tied to the stock market. This makes it a bit different from the other annuity contract types because it is the only contract where your money is subject to losses because of market declines. Your contract value has a greater opportunity to grow, but it also stands to lose. Additionally, your contract's value will be subject to the underlying investment's fees and limitations—including capital gains taxes, management fees, etc. Once it is time for you to receive income from the contract, the insurance company will pay you a certain income, locked in at whatever your contract's value was.

Fixed

A traditional fixed annuity is pretty straightforward. You purchase a contract with a guaranteed interest rate and, when you are ready, the insurance company will make regular income payments to you at whatever payout rate your contract guarantees. Those payments will continue for the rest of your life and, if you choose, for the remainder of your spouse's life.

Fixed annuities don't typically offer significant upside potential, but many people like them for their guarantees (after all, if your Aunt May lives to be ninety-five, knowing she has a paycheck later in life can be her mental and financial safety net), as well as for their predictability. Unlike variable annuities, which are subject to market risk and might be up one year and down the next, you can easily calculate the value of your fixed annuity over your lifetime.

Fixed Index

To recap, variable annuities take on more risk to offer more possibilities to grow. Fixed annuities have less potential growth, but they protect your principal. In the last couple of decades, many insurance companies have retooled their product line to offer fixed index annuities, which are sort of midway between variable and fixed annuities on that risk/reward spectrum. Fixed index annuities offer greater growth potential than traditional fixed annuities but less than variable annuities. Like traditional fixed annuities, however, fixed index annuities are protected from downside market losses.

Fixed index annuities earn interest that is tied to an external market index, meaning that, instead of your contract value growing at a set interest rate like a traditional fixed annuity, it has the potential to grow within a range. Your contract's value is credited interest based on the performance of an external market index like the S&P 500 while never being invested in the market itself. You can't invest in the S&P 500 directly, but each year, your annuity as the potential to earn interest based on the chosen index's performance, subject to limits set by the company such as caps, spreads and participation rates. For instance, if your contract caps your interest at 5 percent, then in a year that the S&P 500 gains 3 percent, your annuity value increases 3 percent. If the S&P 500 gains 35 percent, your annuity value gets a 5 percent interest bump. But since your money isn't actually invested in the market with a fixed index annuity, if the market nosedives (such as happened during 2000, 2008, 2020, and 2022, anyone?) you won't see any increase in your contract value. Conversely, there will also be no decrease in your contract value—no matter how badly the market performed, as long as you follow the terms of the contract, you won't lose any of the interest you were credited in previous years.

So, what if the S&P 500 shows a market loss of 30 percent? Your contract value isn't going anywhere (unless you purchased an optional rider—this charge will still come out of your annuity value each year). For those who are more interested in protection than growth potential, fixed index annuities can be an attractive option because, when the stock market has a long period of positive performance, a fixed index annuity can enjoy conservative growth. And, during stretches where the stock market is erratic and stock values across the board take significant losses? Fixed index annuities won't lose anything due to the stock market volatility.

In my experience, these words immediately elicit a look of concern from a client: annuities, life insurance, and reverse mortgage. I find this initial concern fascinating and am always curious about what causes this reaction. Often, it's because they read a bad article. Maybe they saw a commercial featuring a celebrity they don't trust or their neighbor told them a horror story about someone who had a bad experience.

There are definitely some bad apples out there, but just like everything else in life, there are two sides to every story. My goal is to ensure you have the most accurate information to make your own decisions regardless of what others think or say.

Headlines attached to stories about financial situations can sometimes prove alarming just to pique interest. For example, I might raise an eyebrow if a headline is critical of reverse mortgages since my team and I work with many retirees who choose a reverse mortgage. What I might find, though, if I read through the entire article is that at the end, the writer briefly notes that the couple in question had not paid property taxes in several years. Whether you have a traditional, reverse, or even no mortgage, what would happen if you did not pay your property taxes to the city or municipality where you live? We all know the answer, and it has nothing to do with the mortgage.

Annuities and other tools get similar bad, undeserved reputations because people don't take the time to understand how these tools really work. They make a snap judgment based on someone else's opinion or bad experience and decide it's not for them. If you're willing to keep an open mind, I am willing to share some thoughts and ideas on the topics, and while they're not for everyone, they certainly can be used as a compliment in many retirement plans.

Other Things to Know About Annuities

We just talked about the four kinds of annuity contracts available, but all of them have some commonalities as annuities.

For all annuities, the contractual guarantees are only as strong as the insurance company that sells the product, which makes it important to thoroughly check the credit ratings of any company whose products you are considering.

Annuities are tax-deferred, meaning you don't have to pay taxes on interest earnings each year as the contract value grows. Instead, you will pay ordinary income taxes on your withdrawals. These are meant to be long-term products, so, like other tax-deferred or tax-advantaged products, if you begin taking withdrawals from your contract before age fifty-nine-and-one-half, you may also have to pay a 10 percent federal tax penalty. Also, while annuities are generally considered illiquid, most contracts allow you to withdraw up to 10 percent of your contract value every year. Withdraw any more, however, and you could incur additional surrender penalties.

Keep in mind, your withdrawals will deplete the accumulated cash value, death benefit, and, possibly, the rider values of your contract.

What if I told you we could use a fixed or fixed indexed annuity to help you solve for sequence of return risk?

If, by unfortunate circumstance and timing, you retired into a multi-year bear market or recession, can the allocation of all of your investment and retirement assets sustain severe market losses in the first one, two, or three years of your retirement? This is really what we're getting at when we talk about sequence of return risk. As you can imagine, this could devastate a twenty, thirty, or forty-year retirement plan, even if you started with the right amount in your nest egg. Can you live on Social Security alone? For most, that is not enough to cover their basic living needs.

Many saw this happen when they retired in early 2000. You may recall that broad markets declined in 2000, 2001, and 2002—referred to as the burst of the dot.com bubble. During that period, the U.S. also experienced one of the worst terrorist attacks in history on September 11, 2001.

From a retiree's perspective, this roiled financial markets even further into negative territory. For example, Jake's parents had built a large nest egg of over $750,000. They had paid off their mortgage before retirement. They bought long-term care policies because Jake's grandmother had dementia, and they saw how this drained the family emotionally and financially. They had a savings account at their credit union with $35,000 for emergencies. They did not have any credit card debt or owe anything on their cars. They did everything right.

The one thing they didn't plan for was starting the first three years of a twenty to thirty-year retirement generating sizable losses in their nest egg. In addition to the investment losses, Jake's parents were drawing about $2,500 per month out of their portfolio, which only represented a 4 percent distribution rate ($30,000 per year out of $750,000). That was a reasonable plan at the time, but let's do some simple math. Over those first three years, Jake's parents stuck to their plan and continued drawing out $30,000 per year ($120,000 total) to supplement their Social Security checks. Their financial advisor assured them that a 4 percent withdrawal rate was "normal" and would be sustainable (see Chart 1). Their portfolio had a mix of stocks and bonds, and it seemed like a reasonable and balanced plan for a newly retired couple in their mid-sixties. However, an assumption that accompanied this analysis was that the rate of return would be a flat 5 percent.

However, their portfolio experienced 6, 9, and 15 percent losses over the same three years. By the end of 2002, their portfolio was now worth about $475,000.

The problem is that they are only starting their fourth year of retirement, and they still need the $30,000 per year from their portfolio. This now represents a draw rate of about 6.3 percent per year rather than the 4 percent draw rate they started at. Their nest egg will not last anywhere close to what was anticipated if they continue drawing out the same $2,500 per month (see Chart 2). Jake's dad made the tough decision to return to work part-time for about ten years and lower the draw they needed from their portfolio. He knew that if he didn't change something, there was a good likelihood that they could run out of money. His biggest fear was dying sooner and leaving this risk on his wife, whose family had longevity on their side. It was not an easy decision, but it was one of a few options on the table.

Who controls this? No one; it is pure chance. In *The Psychology of Money*, author Morgan Housel states that luck and risk are siblings. Unfortunately, Jake's parents landed on the risk side of that coin flip.

The good news is that you *can* plan for this. Jake was determined not to let this happen to him and created a retirement income plan that integrated the possibility of bad markets or recessions early in his retirement. Jake's plan incorporated a fixed index annuity for part of his overall asset allocation as using these annuities is a solid way retirees can plan for the bad side of sequence of return risk.

I hope you always land on the "luck" side of the coin flip, but we should still plan for the "risk" side, just in case.

Chart 1: Balance by Year

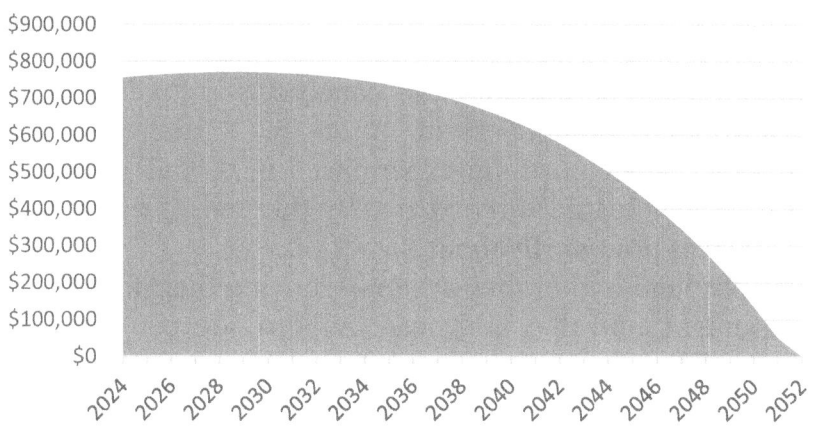

Chart 1

Time before depletion of funds: 28 years, 7 months
Starting retirement balance: $750,000
Rate of return: 5 percent
Withdrawals: Monthly, with 4 percent annual increase for inflation

Results Summary

Cumulative savings at retirement	$750,000
Amount you want to spend annually in retirement	$30,000 ($2,500 /month)
Expected inflation rate	4%
After tax rate of return in retirement	5%
Total investment earnings	$827,205
Total withdrawals	$1,577,205

Retirement Savings Balance by Year

Year	Starting Balance	Withdrawals	Investment Earnings	Ending Balance
2023	$750,000	$30,546	$36,684	$756,138
2024	$756,138	$31,768	$36,958	$761,328
2025	$761,328	$33,039	$37,184	$765,473
2026	$765,473	$34,360	$37,356	$768,468
2027	$768,468	$35,735	$37,469	$770,202
2028	$770,202	$37,164	$37,517	$770,555
2029	$770,555	$38,651	$37,495	$769,400
2030	$769,400	$40,197	$37,396	$766,599
2031	$766,599	$41,804	$37,213	$762,008
2032	$762,008	$43,477	$36,939	$755,470
2033	$755,470	$45,216	$36,565	$746,820
2034	$746,820	$47,024	$36,085	$735,880
2035	$735,880	$48,905	$35,487	$722,462
2036	$722,462	$50,862	$34,764	$706,364
2037	$706,364	$52,896	$33,905	$687,373
2038	$687,373	$55,012	$32,899	$665,260
2039	$665,260	$57,212	$31,734	$639,782
2040	$639,782	$59,501	$30,399	$610,681
2041	$610,681	$61,881	$28,881	$577,681
2042	$577,681	$64,356	$27,165	$540,489
2043	$540,489	$66,930	$25,236	$498,795
2044	$498,795	$69,607	$23,080	$452,268
2045	$452,268	$72,392	$20,679	$400,555
2046	$400,555	$75,287	$18,016	$343,284
2047	$343,284	$78,299	$15,072	$280,057
2048	$280,057	$81,431	$11,827	$210,453
2049	$210,453	$84,688	$8,260	$134,025
2050	$134,025	$88,076	$4,348	$50,297
2051	$50,297	$50,890	$593	$0

Source: dinkytown.net/java/how-long-will-my-retirement-savings-last.html

Chart 2: Balance by Year

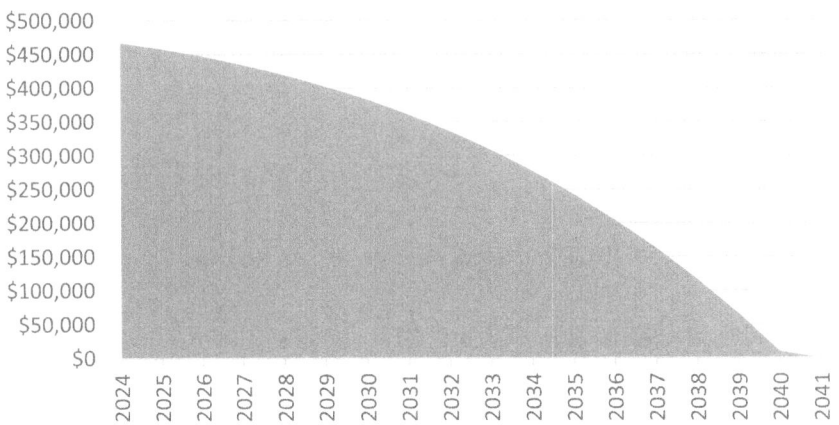

Chart 2

Time before depletion of funds: 17 years, 2 months
Starting retirement balance: $475,000
Rate of return: 5 percent
Withdrawals: Monthly, with 4 percent annual increase for inflation

Results Summary

Cumulative savings at retirement	$475,000
Amount you want to spend annually in retirement	$30,000 ($2,500 /month)
Expected inflation rate	4%
After tax rate of return in retirement	5%
Total investment earnings	$258,363
Total withdrawals	$733,363

Note: Hypothetical example.

Retirement Savings Balance by Year

Year	Starting Balance	Withdrawals	Investment Earnings	Ending Balance
2023	$475,000	$30,546	$22,934	$467,388
2024	$467,388	$31,768	$22,521	$458,140
2025	$458,140	$33,039	$22,024	$447,126
2026	$447,126	$34,360	$21,438	$434,204
2027	$434,204	$35,735	$20,755	$419,225
2028	$419,225	$37,164	$19,968	$402,029
2029	$402,029	$38,651	$19,069	$382,447
2030	$382,447	$40,197	$18,048	$360,299
2031	$360,299	$41,804	$16,898	$335,392
2032	$335,392	$43,477	$15,608	$307,524
2033	$307,524	$45,216	$14,168	$276,476
2034	$276,476	$47,024	$12,567	$242,019
2035	$242,019	$48,905	$10,794	$203,908
2036	$203,908	$50,862	$8,836	$161,883
2037	$161,883	$52,896	$6,681	$115,668
2038	$115,668	$55,012	$4,314	$64,970
2039	$64,970	$57,212	$1,720	$9,477
2040	$9,477	$9,496	$19	$0

Source: *dinkytown.net/java/how-long-will-my-retirement-savings-last.html*

Annuities aren't for everyone, but it's important to understand them before saying "yea" or "nay" on whether they fit into your plan; otherwise, you're not operating with complete information, wouldn't you agree? Regardless, you should talk to a financial professional who can help you understand annuities, help you dissect your particular financial needs, and help show you whether an annuity is appropriate for your retirement income plan.

CHAPTER 8
Estate & Legacy

I n my practice, I devote a significant portion of my time to matters of estates. That doesn't mean drawing up wills or trusts or putting together powers of attorney or anything like that. After all, I'm not an estate planning attorney. But I am a financial professional, and what part of the "estate" isn't affected by money matters?

I've included this chapter because I have seen many people do estate planning wrong. Clients, or clients' families, have come in after experiencing a death in the family and have found themselves in the middle of probate, high taxes, or a discovery of something unforeseen (often long-term care) draining the estate.

I have also seen people do estate planning right: clients or families who visit my office to talk about legacies and how to make them last and adult children who have room to grieve without an added burden of unintended costs, without stress from a family ruptured because of inadequate planning.

I'll share some of these stories here. However, I'm not going to give you specific advice, since everyone's situation is unique. I only want to give you some things to think about and to underscore the importance of planning ahead.

You Can't Take It With You

When it comes to legacy and estate planning, the most important thing is to *do it*. I have heard people from clients to celebrities (rap artist Snoop Dogg comes to mind) say they aren't interested in what happens to their assets when they die because they'll be dead. That's certainly one way to look at it. But I think that's a very selfish way to go about things—we all have people and causes we care about, and those who care about us. Even if the people we love don't *need* what we leave behind, they can still be fined or legally tied up in the probate process or burial costs if we don't plan for those. And that's not even considering what happens if you become incapacitated at some point while you are still alive. Having a plan in place can greatly reduce the stress of those responsibilities on your loved ones; it's just a loving thing to do.

Documents

There are a few documents that lay the groundwork of legacy planning. You've probably heard of all or most of them, but I'd like to review what they are and how people commonly use them. These are all things you should talk about with an estate planning attorney to establish your legacy.

Powers of Attorney

A power of attorney, or POA, is a document giving someone the authority to act on your behalf and in your best interests. These come in handy in situations where you cannot be present (think a vacation where you get stuck in Canada) or, for durable powers of attorney, even when you are incapacitated (think in a coma or coping with dementia).

It is important to have powers of attorney in place and to appoint someone you trust to act on your behalf in these matters. Have you ever heard of someone who was incapacitated after a car accident, whether from head trauma or being in a coma for weeks—sometimes months? Do you think their bills stopped coming due during that time? I like my phone company and my bank, but neither one is about to put a moratorium on sending me bills, particularly not for an extended or interminable period. A power of attorney would have the authority to pay your mortgage or cancel your cable while you are unable.

You can have multiple POAs and require them to act jointly.

What this looks like: Do you think two heads are better than one? One man, Chris, significantly relied on his two sons' opinions for both his business and personal matters. He appointed both sons as joint POA, requiring both their signoffs for his medical and financial matters.

You can have multiple POAs who can act independently.

What this looks like: Irene had three children with whom she routinely stayed. They lived in different areas of the country, which she thought was an advantage; one month she might be hiking out West, the next she could enjoy the newest off-Broadway production, and the next she could soak up some Southern sun. She named her three children as independently authorized POAs, so, if something happened, no matter where she was, the child closest could step in to act on her behalf.

You can have POAs who have different responsibilities.

What this looks like: Although Luke's friend Claire, a nurse, was his go-to and POA for health-related issues, financial matters usually made her nervous, so he appointed his good neighbor, Matt, as his POA in all of his financial and legal matters.

In addition to POAs, it may be helpful to have an advanced medical directive. This is a document where you have pre-decided what choices you would make about different health scenarios. An advanced medical directive can help ease the burden for your medical POA and loved ones, particularly when it comes to end-of-life care.

Wills

Perhaps the most basic document of legacy planning, a will is a legal document wherein you outline your wishes for your estate. When it comes to your estate after your death, having a will is the foundation of your legacy. Without one, your loved ones are left behind, guessing what you would have wanted, and the court will likely split your assets according to the state's defaults. Maybe that's exactly what you wanted, as far as anyone knows, right? Because even if you told your nephew he could have your car he's been driving, if it's not in writing, it still might go to the brother, sister, son, or daughter to whom you aren't speaking.

However, it may not be enough just to have a will. Even with a will, your assets will be subject to probate. Probate is what we call the state's process for determining a will's validity. A judge will go through your will to question if it conflicts with state law, if it is the most up-to-date document, if you were mentally competent at the time it was in order, etc. For some, this is a quick, easily-resolved process. For others, particularly if someone steps forward to contest the will, it may take years to settle, all the while subjecting the assets to court costs and attorney's fees.

One other undesirable piece of the probate process is that it is a public process. That means anyone can go to the courthouse, ask for copies of the case, and discover your assets. They can also see who is slated to receive what and who is disputing.

It's also important to remember that beneficiary lines trump wills. So, that large life insurance policy? What if, when you bought it fifteen years ago, you wrote your ex-husband's name on the beneficiary line? Even if you stipulate otherwise in your will, the company that holds your policy will pay out to your ex-spouse. Or, how about the thousands of dollars in your IRA you dedicated to the children thirty years ago, but one of your children was killed in a car accident, leaving his wife and two toddlers behind? That IRA is going to transfer to your remaining children, with nothing for your daughter-in-law and grandchildren.

That may paint a grim portrait, but I can't underscore enough the importance of working with a skilled estate planning attorney to keep your will and beneficiary lines up to date as your life changes.

Generally, your will should be considered an overflow document to cast a wide net over any assets that are in your name for which you can't or haven't officially designated a beneficiary. Examples may include a vehicle, the items and furniture that fill your home, or a family heirloom that has been passed down from one generation to the next. There are generally no beneficiary forms for these types of assets, in which case a will is very important.

You should review your beneficiary forms for all retirement and investment accounts every few years at a minimum—certainly more frequently if and when a life event happens. Death, divorce, a job change, or asset rollovers from one custodian to another are all good times to revisit your beneficiary documents.

Trusts

Another piece of legacy planning to consider is the trust.

A trust is set up through an attorney and allows a third party, or trustee, to hold your assets and determine how they will pass to your beneficiaries. Many people are skeptical of trusts because they assume trusts are only appropriate for the fabulously wealthy.

However, a simple trust will likely cost more than $1,000 if prepared by an attorney and fees can be higher for couples.[47] But a trust can help you avoid both the expense and publicity of probate, provide a more immediate transfer of wealth, avoid some taxes, and provide you greater control over your legacy.

For instance, if you want to set aside some funds for a grandchild's college education, you can make it a requirement he or she enrolls in classes before your trust will dispense any funds. Like a will, beneficiary lines will override your trust conditions, so you must still keep insurance policies and other assets up to date.

Like any financial or legal consideration, there are many options these days beyond the simple "yes or no" question of whether to have a trust. For one thing, you will need to consider if you want your trust to be revocable (you can change the terms while you are alive) or irrevocable (can't be changed; you are no longer the "owner" of the contents). A brief note here about irrevocable trusts: Although they have significant and greater tax benefits, they are still subject to a Medicaid look-back period. This means, if you transfer your assets into an irrevocable trust in an attempt to shelter them from a Medicaid spend-down, you will be ineligible for Medicaid coverage of long-term care for five years. Yet, an irrevocable trust can avoid both probate and estate taxes, and it can even protect assets from legal judgments against you.

Another thing to remember when it comes to trusts, in general, is, even if you have set up a trust, you must remember to fund it. In my twenty-plus years' work, I've had numerous clients come to me, assuming they have protected their assets with a trust. When we talk about taxes and other pieces of their legacy, it turns out they never retitled any assets or changed any paperwork on the assets they wanted in the trust. So, please

---

[47] Rickie Houston. smartasset.com. August 31, 2022. "How Much Does It Cost to Set Up a Trust? https://smartasset.com/estate-planning/how-much-does-it-cost-to-set-up-a-trust

remember, a trust is just a bunch of fancy legal papers if you haven't followed through on retitling your assets.

Taxes

Although charitable contributions, trusts, and other tax-efficient strategies can reduce your tax bill, it's unlikely your estate will be passed on entirely tax-free. Yet, when it comes to building a legacy that can last for generations, taxes can be one of the heaviest drains on the impact of your hard work.

For 2023, the federal estate exemption was $12.92 million per individual and $25.84 million for a married couple, with estates facing up to a 40 percent tax rate after that. Currently, the new estate limits are set to increase with inflation until January 1, 2026, when they will "sunset" back to the inflation-adjusted 2017 limits.[48] And that's not taking into account the various state regulations and taxes regarding estate and inheritance transfers.

Another tax concern "frequent flyer": retirement accounts.

Your IRA or 401(k) can be a source of tax issues when you pass away. For one thing, taking funds from a sizeable account can trigger a large tax bill. However, if you leave the assets in the account, there are still required minimum distributions (RMDs), which will take effect even after you die. If you pass the account to your spouse, he or she can keep taking your RMDs as is, or your spouse can retitle the account in his or her name and receive RMDs based on his or her life expectancy. Remember, if you don't take your RMDs, the IRS will take up to 25 percent of your required distribution (10 percent if corrections are made in a timely fashion). You will still have to pay income taxes whenever you withdraw that money. Provisions in the original SECURE Act, anyone who inherits your IRA, with few exceptions (your spouse, a beneficiary less

---

[48] IRS.gov. December 20, 2022. "What's New — Estate and Gift Tax" https://www.irs.gov/businesses/small-businesses-self-employed/whats-new-estate-and-gift-tax

than ten years younger, or a disabled adult child, to name a few), will need to empty the account within ten years of your death.

Also—and this is a pretty big also—check with an attorney if you are considering putting your IRA or 401(k) in a trust. An improperly titled beneficiary form for the IRA could mean the difference of thousands of dollars in taxes. This is just one more reason to work with a financial professional, one who can strategically partner with an estate planning attorney to diligently check your decisions.

CHAPTER 9

Women Retire Too

I help men, women, and families from all walks of life on their journey to and through retirement. Yet, we want to address the female demographic specifically. Why? To be perfectly blunt, women are more likely to deal with poverty than men when they reach retirement.

In 2021, the overall poverty rate for women slightly exceeded the rate for men, but among those seventy-five years and older, 13.51 percent of women lived at the poverty rate compared to 8.82 percent of men.[49]

The topics, products, and strategies I cover elsewhere in this book are meant to help address retirement concerns for men *and* women, but the dire statistic above is a reminder that much of traditional planning is geared toward men. Male careers, male lifespans, male health care. The bottom line is women's career paths often look much different than men's, so why would their retirement planning look the same?

Women often embrace different roles and values than men as workers, wives, mothers, and daughters. They are more apt to take on roles as caretakers. They often plan for events, worry about loved ones, tend to details, and think about the future. Also, they often want everything to be just right, and they want

---

49 statistica.com. 2023. "Poverty rate in the United States in 2021, by age and gender" https://www.statista.com/statistics/233154/us-poverty-rate-by-gender/

to be right themselves. It could be you've seen the following affixed to a decorative sign, refrigerator magnet, or T-shirt: "If I agreed with you, we'd both be wrong." The barb features a picture of a woman speaking to a man.

If these characteristics I listed about women are accurate, shouldn't they deserve special considerations from financial professionals? The case can be made, particularly since 69 percent of men in the U.S. age 65 and older happen to be married, compared to 47 percent of women in that age classification.[50] Single women don't have the opportunity to capitalize on the resource pooling and potential economies of scale accompanying a marriage or partnership.

Be Informed

It's a familiar scene in many financial offices across the country: A woman comes into an appointment carrying a sack full of unopened envelopes. Often through tears, she sits across the desk from a financial professional and apologizes her way through a conversation about what financial products she owns and where her income is coming from. She is recently widowed and was sure her spouse was taking care of the finances, but now she doesn't know where all their assets are kept, and her confidence in her financial outlook has wavered after walking through funeral expenses and realizing she's down to one income.

Often, she may be financially "okay." Yet, the uncertainty can be wearying, particularly when the family is already reeling from a loss. While this scenario sometimes plays out with men, in my experience, it's more likely to be a woman in that chair across from my desk, probably, in part, because of Western traditions about money management being "a guy thing." But

---

[50] Administration for Community Living. November 30, 2022. "Profile of Older Americans." https://acl.gov/aging-and-disability-in-america/data-and-research/profile-older-americans

it doesn't have to be this way. This all-too-common scenario can be wiped away with just a little preparation.

Talk to Your Spouse/ Work with a Financial Professional

While there are many factors affecting women's financial preparation for and situation in retirement, I cannot emphasize enough that the decision to be informed, to be a part of the conversation, and to be aware of what is going on with your finances is absolutely paramount to a confident retirement.

With all the couples I've seen, there is almost always an "alpha" when it comes to finances. It isn't always men—for many of my coupled clients, the wife is the alpha who keeps the books and budgets and knows where all of the family's assets are, down to the penny—yet, statistically, among baby boomers it is usually a man who runs the books. But, as time goes on, it looks like the ratio of male to female financial alphas is evening out based on my experience speaking with couples.

The breakdown happens when there is a lack of communication, when no one other than the financial alpha knows how much the family has and where. In the end, it doesn't matter who handles the money; it's about all parties being informed of what's going on financially.

A woman once commented to me that to get this conversation rolling, she asked her husband "to teach her how to be a widow." They spent a day, just one part of an otherwise dull weekend, going through everything she might need to know. They spent the better part of two decades together after that. When he died, and she was widowed, she said the "widowhood" talk had made a huge difference. She knew who to call to talk through their retirement plan and where to call for the insurance policy.

She said the fruit of the weekend exercise they engaged in some twenty years earlier couldn't have been more apparent than when she ultimately accompanied a recently widowed friend of hers to a financial appointment. Her friend was emotional the whole time, afraid she would run out of money any day. The financial professional ultimately showed the friend that she was financially in good shape, but not before the friend had already spent months worried that each check would exhaust her bank account. That's no way to live after losing a loved one. It was preventable had her deceased spouse and financial professional included her in a conversation about "widowhood."

Spouse-Specific Options

One area where it might be especially important to be on the same page between spouses is when it comes to financial products or services that have spousal options. A few that come to mind are pensions and Social Security, although life insurance and annuity policies also have the potential to affect both spouses.

With pensions, taking the worker's life-only option is somewhat attractive—after all, the monthly payment is bigger. However, you and your spouse should discuss your options. When we're talking about both of you, as opposed to just one lifespan, there is an increased likelihood at least one of you will live a long, long time. This means the monthly payout will be less, but it also ensures that, no matter which spouse outlives the other, no one will have to suffer the loss of a needed pension paycheck in his or her later retirement years.

While we covered Social Security options in a different chapter, I think some of the spousal information bears repeating. Particularly, if you worked exclusively inside the home for a significant number of years, you may want to talk about taking your Social Security benefits based on your spouse's work history. After all, Social Security is based on your thirty-five highest-earning years.

Things to remember about the spousal benefits:[51]

- Your benefit will be calculated as a percentage (up to 50 percent) of your spouse's earned monthly benefit at his or her full retirement age, or FRA.
- For you to begin receiving a spousal benefit, your spouse must have already filed for his or her own benefits and you must be at least sixty-two.
- You can qualify for a full half of your spouse's benefits if you wait until you reach FRA to file.
- Beginning your benefits earlier than your FRA will reduce your monthly check but waiting to file until after FRA will not increase your benefits.

For divorcees:[52]

- You may qualify for an ex-spousal benefit if . . .
  a. You were married for a decade or more
  b. *and* you are at least sixty-two
  c. *and* you have been divorced for at least two years
  d. *and* you are currently unmarried
  e. *and* your ex-spouse is sixty-two (qualifies to begin taking Social Security)
- Your ex-spouse does not need to have filed for you to file on his or her benefit.
- Similar to spousal benefits, you can qualify for up to half of your ex-spouse's benefits if you wait to file until your FRA.
- If your ex-spouse dies, you may file to receive a widow/widower benefit on his or her Social Security record as long as you are at least age sixty and fulfill all the other requirements on the preceding alphabetized list.

---

[51] Social Security Administration. "Retirement Planner: Benefits For You As A Spouse." https://www.ssa.gov/planners/retire/applying6.html
[52] Social Security Administration. "Retirement Planner: If You Are Divorced." https://www.ssa.gov/planners/retire/divspouse.html

    a. This will not affect the benefits of your ex-spouse's current spouse

For widow's (or widower's, for that matter) benefits:[53]

- You may qualify to receive as much as your deceased spouse would have received if . . .
    a. You were married for at least nine months before his or her death
    b. *or* you would qualify for a divorced spousal benefit
    c. *and* you are at least sixty
    d. *and* you did not/have not remarried before age sixty
- You may earn delayed credits on your spouse's benefit *if* your spouse hadn't already filed for benefits when he or she died.
- Other rules may apply to you if you are disabled or are caring for a deceased spouse's dependent or disabled child.

Longevity

On average, women live longer than men. Most stats put average female longevity at about two years more than men. But averages are tricky things. An April 2022 report by the World Economic Forum listed the eight oldest people in the world to all be women. They ranged in age from 114 to 118 years old and included two Americans.[54]

On one hand, this is a Brandi Chastain moment. You know, when the American soccer icon shed her jersey to celebrate a

[53] Social Security Administration. "Survivors Planner: If You Are The Worker's Widow Or Widower."
https://www.ssa.gov/planners/survivors/ifyou.html#h2

[54] Martin Armstrong. World Economic Forum. April 29, 2022. "How old are the world's oldest people?"
https://www.weforum.org/agenda/2022/04/the-oldest-people-in-the-world/

game-winning penalty kick to win the World Cup. Seriously, how fabulous are women? They tend to be meticulous, resolute, and perseverant. On the other hand, the trend for women to live longer presents longstanding financial ramifications.

Simply Needing More Money in Retirement

Living longer in retirement means needing more money, period. Barring a huge lottery win or some crazy stock market action, the date you retire is likely the point at which you have the most money you will ever have. Not to put too grim a spin on it, but the problem with longevity is, the further you get away from that date, the further your dollars have to stretch. If you planned to live to a nice eighty-something but live to a nice one-hundred-something, that is *two decades* you will need to account for, monetarily.

To put this in perspective, let's say you like to drink coffee as an everyday splurge. Not accounting for inflation or leap years, a $2.50 cup-a-day habit is $18,250 over a two-decade span. Now, think of all the things you like to do that cost money. Add those up for twenty years of unanticipated costs. I think you'll see what I mean.

During the 2020 onset of the coronavirus pandemic, many learned to cut costs. For some, that amounted to skipping their decadent latte. For others, however, cutbacks became acute. According to data compiled by Age Wave and Edward Jones, 32 percent of Americans plan to retire later than planned because of the pandemic. Women felt a more adverse effect. The report stipulated that 41 percent of women continued to save for retirement, compared to 58 percent of men.[55]

---

[55] Megan Leonhardt. cnbc.com. June 16, 2021. "58% of men were able to continue saving for retirement during the pandemic—but only 41% of women were." https://www.cnbc.com/2021/06/16/why-pandemic-hit-womens-retirement-savings-more-than-mens.html

More Health Care Needs

In addition to the cost of living for a longer lifespan is the fact aging, plain and simple, means more health care, and more health care means more money. Women are survivors. They suffer from the morbidity-mortality paradox, which states women suffer more non-fatal illnesses throughout their lifetime than men, who experience fewer illnesses but higher mortality.

Women have been found to seek treatment more often when not feeling well and emphasize staying healthy when older, according to studies. Survival, I believe, is on the side of the woman. However, surviving things, like cancer, also means more checkups later in life.

A statistical concern for women involves the prospect of long-term care. Long-term care for women lasts 3.7 years on average compared to 2.2 years for men.[56]

Widowhood

Not only do women typically live longer than their same-age male counterparts, they also stand a greater chance of living alone as they age. Some divorce, separate or never marry. Among those age sixty-five and over, 33 percent of women live alone compared to 20 percent of men.[57]

I don't write this to scare people; rather, I think it's fundamentally important to prepare my female clients for something that may be a startling, *but very likely,* scenario. At some point, most women will have to handle their financial situations on their own. A little preparation can go a long way,

---

[56] Lindsay Modglin. singlecare.com. February 15, 2022. "Long-term care statistics 2022" https://www.singlecare.com/blog/news/long-term-care-statistics/

[57] statistica.com. November 23, 2022. "Share of senior households living alone in the United States 2020, by gender" https://www.statista.com/statistics/912400/senior-households-living-alone-usa/

l

and having a basic understanding of your household finances and the "who, what, where, and how much" of your family's assets is incredibly useful—it can prevent a tragic situation from being more traumatic.

In my opinion, the financial services industry sometimes underserves women in these situations. Some financial professionals tend to alienate women, even when their spouses are alive. I've heard several stories of women who sat through meeting after meeting without their financial professional ever addressing a single question to them.

In our firm, when we work with couples, we work hard to make sure our retirement income strategies work for *both* people. No matter who the financial alpha is, it's important for everyone affected by a retirement strategy to understand it.

Taxes

One of the often-unexpected aspects of widowhood is the tax bill. Many women continue similar lifestyles to the ones they shared with their spouses. This, in turn, means continuing to have a similar need for income. However, after the death of a spouse, their taxes will be calculated based on a single filer's income table, which is much less forgiving than the couple's tax rates. With proper planning, your financial professional and tax advisor may be able to help you take the sting out of your new tax status.

Caregiving

Caregiving.org updates its national report about every five years. According to its findings released in 2020, of the 53 million caregivers providing unpaid, informal care for older adults, 61 percent are women. Among today's family caregivers,

61 percent work and 45 percent report some kind of financial impact from providing a loved one care and support.[58]

In addition to the financial burden created by caregiving responsibilities, women often devote many hours each day to duties such as housekeeping and looking after loved ones. So then, when can women find the time to focus long and hard on financial matters?

Unfortunately, the impact and hardships created by traditional roles for women typically do not account for Social Security benefit losses or the losses of health care benefits and retirement savings. This also doesn't account for maternity care, mothers who homeschool, or women who leave the workforce to care for their children in any way.

I don't repeat these statistics to scare you. Not only are unpaid family caregivers spending their time and energy taking care of others, but they're also putting their own money towards the cause. An AARP study found that three-quarters of family caregivers surveyed were spending an average of $7,242 a year on out-of-pocket caregiving costs.[59] Yet, I think the emotional value of the care many women provide their elderly relatives or neighbors cannot be quantified. So, to be clear, this shouldn't be taken as a "why not to provide caregiving" spiel. Instead, it should be seen as a call for "why to *prepare* for caregiving" or "how to lessen the financial and emotional burden of caregiving."

Funding Your Own Retirement

For these reasons, women need to be prepared to fund more of their own retirements. There are several savings options and products, including the spousal IRA. Unlike a traditional IRA,

[58] caregiving.org. 2020 Report. "Caregiving in the U.S. 2020."
https://www.caregiving.org/caregiving-in-the-us-2020/
[59] Nancy Kerr. AARP. June 29, 2021. " Family Caregivers Spend More Than $7,200 a Year on Out-of-Pocket Costs."
https://www.aarp.org/caregiving/financial-legal/info-2021/high-out-of-pocket-costs.html

where you contribute money to a plan with your employer, a spousal IRA is something your spouse sets up on your behalf, so he or she can contribute a portion of the paycheck to your retirement funds. This is something to consider, particularly for families where one spouse has dropped out of the workforce to care for a relative.

Also, if you find yourself in a caregiving role, talk to your employer's human resources department. Some companies have paid leave, special circumstance, or sick leave options you could qualify for, making it easier to cope and helping you stay in the workforce longer.

Saving Money

Women need more money to fund their retirements, period. But this doesn't have to be a significant burden—often, women are better at saving, while usually taking less risk in their portfolios.[60] This gives me reason to believe, as women get more involved in their finances, families will continue to be better-prepared for retirement, both *his* and *hers*.

---

[60] Maurie Backman. The Motley Fool. March 4, 2021. "A Summary of 20 Years of Research and Statistics on Women in Investing." https://www.fool.com/research/women-in-investing-research/

CHAPTER 10

Finding a Financial Professional

D o you remember those aptitude tests that supposedly identified the career fields you were most suited for? According to mine, I was best suited for a career in engineering. It made sense; my father was an engineer, after all. Yet, I had dropped out of a work shadow program in the engineering field. The aptitude test was wrong; it turned out I had no interest in engineering. At seventeen, I had no idea what I wanted to do after I graduated, but I knew I was not interested in engineering.

After dropping out of the work shadow program, I became a teacher's aide for Mrs. Patti Shafer's personal finance class. Mrs. Schafer was passionate about teaching kids real-world lessons like how to balance a checkbook, how taxes get taken out of your paycheck, and even how to invest in the stock market—all foreign concepts to my classmates and me.

I'll never forget the day John "GB" Richmond appeared in our classroom as a guest speaker. He was probably in his late twenties and a very engaging speaker. What stuck with me the most was when he talked about compound returns and encouraged us to start saving for retirement as soon as possible. On the projector (yes, we used projectors back then), a slide showed a small classroom of kids on a path to having $1 million. I was blown away. What was this magic, and why had no one ever taught me about it before? At the end of his presentation, I remember John saying, "Start saving young and never stop."

I made a point to introduce myself to John, and after he left our class, I asked Mrs. Shafer if I could intern at Richmond Brothers for the rest of my senior year. What did I have to lose since I'd already dropped out of the engineering program? I wanted to explore further the topic of compound interest that John had just opened my eyes to.

A few days later, Mrs. Shafer and I called John and his brother, Dave (also his business partner), to ask if they would let me intern for the remainder of the school year. They'd never had an intern and were initially hesitant but eventually agreed. A single presentation in a high school classroom turned into an internship that would turn into a full-blown career in financial services.

While my high school aptitude test had decided I should follow in my father's engineering footsteps, one could argue that I was actually destined for financial services. Allow me to explain.

In 1988 when I was just eight years old, my mother was diagnosed with Lymphoma. Over the next two years, treatments failed, and she passed away at the age of thirty-six, leaving behind her husband (my dad) and three children.

It was a traumatic time for all of us, and all these years later, I'm still working through how this event impacted me at such a young age. Given their relatively young ages at the time, you can imagine that retirement planning was not at the forefront of my parents' minds. My question for you, dear reader, is: Do you think my dad would have been less stressed about life, finances, and the trauma of losing his wife if someone had told them how important financial planning was for their future? How something like life insurance, even at their age, could be used to protect their family? I bet so. In fact, I know so.

Money does not take away from the loss of a loved one, but it can surely help not to pile on additional financial stress. Medical bills can be an enormous burden for years (decades even) after losing a loved one, yet the mortgage or gas bills keep coming every month.

In my twenty-plus years as a financial advisor, I have seen many unfortunate family circumstances like the one I lived through. Never once has a surviving spouse said, "Matt, all this life insurance money is too much. I don't know what I am going to do with it all."

I am not taking away from the emotional trauma of losing a loved one, but what if you could have taken this simple step for yourself and your family just in case something did happen to you? Imagine the weight lifted if they could focus on grieving instead of sudden financial uncertainty. Financial planning is much more than amassing a big pile of money. It's also about the "what-ifs" life throws at us. It's about hoping for the best but planning for the worst, just in case.

Luckily, my dad found love again and married a wonderful woman I have called Mom for over thirty years. She helped usher me through my teenage and young adult years and has been a tremendous source of inspiration and support for my siblings and me. She retired at sixty-four, while my dad worked a few more years before retiring.

However, life struck again, and my second mom was diagnosed with primary progressive aphasia in her late sixties. As I had worked with my parents on their retirement planning, one critical piece my mom always talked about and wanted to plan for was "what if" one of them became chronically ill. She had retired from working in human resources at a retirement home in Michigan. She was very aware of this risk and wanted to have options.

Not pretending this risk doesn't exist is one form of planning, believe it or not. Many people have difficulty accepting this possibility and therefore do not plan for this "what if." My mom knew all too well how much her residents were spending monthly and yearly on health care, which was scary. My parents got quotes for long-term care policies, and at the time, these costs were outrageous and a poor fit for their plan. Together, we explored a third option that ultimately suited them well. We set up "hybrid" life insurance policies in retirement for each of them.

It is a common thought process that when someone retires, they no longer need life insurance. Hopefully, their kids are grown and out of the house. Generally, any debt or liabilities (such as cars or mortgage debt) are paid down or paid off, and you have your nest egg. "So why do I need life insurance?" they ask. I would like to rephrase this question: What if there was a way to creatively use life insurance in retirement to help cover the risk of chronic illness? More than half of the American population suffers from at least one chronic illness.[61]

Even if you are one of the lucky ones who never have to live through chronic illness, there is a 100 percent chance that we will all face death. Special types of life insurance policies can help with both risks.

My early experience of losing my mother at a young age and watching my father struggle left a more profound impression than I knew. When I discovered the financial services industry and began learning about the tools and resources that can help shield families from potential disaster, there was no other road I could have taken.

As I write this book, I still work for Richmond Brother, Inc.; however, I was fortunate to have the opportunity to buy into the firm when John decided to change careers later in his life. Over the years, I have seen clients through some of their best and worst times. I've been right there with them through the good years with a stable market and good economy, and through the bad years of bear markets and recessions. In those early days, my passion was to have that $1 million to my name—just like John had shown in his presentation. Since then, my passion has evolved greatly. It's not about me anymore; it's about sharing

---

[61] David Hoffman. National Association of Chronic Disease Directors. 2022. "Commentary on Chronic Disease Prevention in 2022" chrome-extension://efaidnbmnnnibpcajpcglclefindmkaj/https://chronicdisease.org/wp-content/uploads/2022/04/FS_ChronicDiseaseCommentary2022FINAL.pdf

the knowledge, tools, and resources my team and I have gathered. My mission is to educate, inform, and guide my clients on their financial and retirement journey no matter what the world puts in our path. That's why I've chosen to write this book. I hope it has empowered you to take control of your financial future so you can be fearless and live your best life today and in retirement. You deserve it.

Acknowledgments

I would like to thank my business partners, Dave Richmond and Tara Furnas. They have shared in the ups and downs of life and business with me for many years and, through it all, continue to be a major source of support and inspiration to me. I love the team approach we have cultivated together with an aim to make a difference in the lives of others.

I'd like to thank all my team members at Richmond Brothers who are on the front lines, working with and helping our clients each and every single day. You inspire me. I'd like to thank my close friends (you know who you are) who have had faith, trust, and confidence in me from day one and continue to support me to this day.

Libby, you have been and continue to be my person in life, and I cherish the relationship we have.

I'd like to thank all of our clients at Richmond Brothers. Working for you and helping guide you through any of life's financial and non-financial circumstances is my great honor.

Lastly, I'd like to thank my husband, Jason. You are an amazing source of support for me always no matter what life throws our way. You create such an amazing, calm, and relaxing space that we call home. In this relaxing space is where I do all my writing and I couldn't have done this without you.

About the Author

MATTHEW J. CURFMAN, CFP®
CEO and Co-Owner
Richmond Brothers, Inc.

As the CEO and Co-Owner of Richmond Brother, Inc., Matt is focused on helping clients work toward their retirement dreams through a well-thought-out strategy for retirement income.

Matt started in the industry in 1998 as an intern for Richmond Brothers. He truly enjoys helping people maintain, use, and grow their wealth so they may pay it forward to their family, friends, and communities.

Matt is securities licensed, has received his CERTIFIED FINANCIAL PLANNER™ certification, and has been a member of Ed Slott's Master Elite IRA Advisor Group™ for over ten years. He graduated in the top 10 percent of his class at Eastern Michigan University.

Matt stars in Richmond Brothers' monthly video segment, "Matt's Minutes," and was featured in *Jackson Magazine's* "30 And Under" Class of 2009. He has contributed to articles featured in *USA Today*, *The Wall Street Journal*, *MarketWatch*, and *The Fiscal Times*, among others.

Matt has served as the chief volunteer officer of the Jackson YMCA and supports the YMCA's "Strong Kids, Strong Communities" campaign. He has served on the American Cancer Society's Tony Open Golf committee, been active as an ACS Relay for Life team member, and is an active sponsor of The Lingap Children's Foundation.

In his free time, Matt enjoys walking his dog, Parker. He also enjoys physical activities such as running, biking, rollerblading, weight lifting, and hiking. Additional hobbies include reading and being outdoors. Last but certainly not least, he cherishes spending time with his spouse and life partner, Jason Cure. They are currently involved in renovating an almost 100-year-old brick Tudor-style home that they hope to move into eventually.

Made in the USA
Middletown, DE
27 September 2023

39434503R00080